When Stories Come to School

WHEN STORIES COME TO SCHOOL

Telling, Writing, and Performing Stories

in the Early Childhood Classroom

by Patsy Cooper

Teachers & Writers Collaborative

New York

When Stories Come to School

Funding for this publication has been provided, in part, by the National Endowment for the Arts and the New York State Council on the Arts. Teachers & Writers also receives funding from the following foundations and corporations: American Stock Exchange, The Bingham Trust, Booth Ferris Foundation, Chemical Bank, Consolidated Edison, Aaron Diamond Foundation, Morgan Stanley Foundation, New York Telephone, New York Times Company Foundation, Henry Nias Foundation, Rotary Foundation of New York, Helena Rubinstein Foundation, and the Scherman Foundation.

Teachers & Writers Collaborative
5 Union Square West
New York, N.Y. 10003–3306

Library of Congress Cataloging-in-Publication Data

Cooper, Patsy.
    When stories come to school : telling, writing, and performing stories in the early childhood classroom / by Patsy Cooper
          p.   cm.
    Includes bibliographical references (p.   )
    ISBN 0-915924-77-3
    1. Storytelling 2. Early childhood education—United States.
I. Title
LB1042.C49   1993
372.64'2—dc20
                                  92-33897
                                    CIP

Design: Chris Edgar
Photos: Monica Rascoe

Printed by Philmark Lithographics, New York, N.Y.
First edition

Table of Contents

To Warren

Acknowledgments

I began my work in schools as a pre-school teacher at Chicago Child Care Society, in Chicago's Hyde Park. There, under the generous guidance of Jean Battle, Shirley Dean, and the teaching staff, I learned that our first duty as teachers is to love "other people's children."[1] In coming to understand this, I saw teaching take on a moral dimension that at once surprised me and changed my life.

From 1982 to 1984, while teaching kindergarten, it was my privilege to be a research assistant in the Erikson Institute Early Literacy Project under the direction of Drs. Gillian D. McNamee and Joan McLane.[2] Our investigation focused on young children's participation in the storytelling and dramatization activities that Vivian Paley described in her inspiring book, *Wally's Stories*. I'd like to express my gratitude, for over ten years later I find myself just as enthralled with the stories young children tell and dramatize. In fact, there seems to be no end to the ways these story activities enhance not only the reading and writing development of young children, but also my own understanding of the young children's development and their never-ending attempt to make sense of the world.

McNamee and McLane further explore early literacy development and storytelling in their book, *Early Literacy*. The authors demonstrate a keen awareness of the relationship between child development and the reading and writing process, an awareness that has been far too absent from the traditional beginning reading and writing curriculum. Also valuable is Paley's *The Boy Who Would Be a Helicopter,* which looks at storytelling from the more personal perspective of one child, Jason, whom Paley describes as the "quintessential outsider."

In 1986, I became the director of Trinity School for Young Children in Houston, Texas. The incredible teachers—among them Connie Floyd, Jennifer Giroux, Carol Heath, Bernie Mathes, Shaundra Simmons, and Mary-o Yeager—and I spent untold hours reviewing the children's stories, as well as their responses to other literacy experiences. A number of teachers in Houston area elementary schools, including Pansy Gee, Margaret Immel, Betsy Thompson, Ilene Schwartz, and Roula Stefanidas, have helped me understand the reading and writing process in the last quarter of early childhood.

In 1988, a generous grant from The Bingham Trust supported the creation of the Early Literacy Outreach Project. I would like to commend, and thank, The Bingham Trust, along with Nancy Larson Shapiro, for its awareness of the potential impact of early childhood education, as well as its patience with our approach, which, like our young storytellers, needed time to take root and mature.

In 1991, the Early Literacy Outreach Project spawned the Teachers' Network for Early Literacy in the Center for Education at Rice University. I'd like to thank Marvin Hoffman, Linda McNeil, and the others at Rice who understand that the stories of our children, not test scores, should be at the center of education.

When you work in schools, so many people come and go with each school year. It's hard to know them all well, but it is easy to be touched by them. At each turn in my work with young children and early literacy development, I've encountered many parents and educators who are dedicated to children, to storytelling, and to reading and writing as an act of real life, and who believe that the classroom teacher can make a real difference. I am grateful for their collective wisdom and support.

Finally, I must thank my two young daughters, Kyle and Jess, who have made me relish story activities not only in their classrooms, but also at home, and ultimately, in the culture they strive to understand through the stories they tell and read.

---

1. Kozol, Jonathan, *Savage Inequalities,* p. 40.
2. McNamee, McLane, Cooper, and Kerwin, "Cognition and Affect in Early Literacy Development," *Early Child Development and Care*, Vol. 20, 1985, pp. 229–244.

Preface

What ought to be interesting . . . is the unfolding of a lived life. . . .

—Robert Coles, *The Call of Stories*

Long before I could read, I learned about reading and writing as a part of real life because of one thing: the newspaper, especially the *Journal American*. Every afternoon I or one of my brothers or sisters was sent around the corner to get the evening edition. Ten cents. There was something beautiful about the stacks of fresh papers, lined up in precise rows on the green wooden stand outside Clark's candy store in the Bronx, a large, lead paperweight holding them down. Though I couldn't read, I could recognize the shape of the words *Journal American*. The thought of mistakenly bringing home the *Herald Tribune* to my waiting parents struck terror in my heart. My parents never talked about access to news, and news from the perspective you liked (not to mention the peace of being alone with one's thoughts), as one of life's more basic pleasures, but somehow we all knew.

Years before I took up teaching, I learned about stories from my sister Julie, when we lay waiting for sleep in the double bed we shared. Julie, three years older than I was, would tell me about whatever book she was reading at the time. She liked mysteries and family stories, and so I did too. Some nights, when Julie was allowed to stay up later than I was, I would sit up in the big bed and look out of the window. I remember being fascinated by the idea of life beyond University and Ogden Avenues, the intersection of our own lives. In the glow of the streetlights below, I could see the buses and taxis rushing out of the neighborhood to what I thought were far-off destinations, making the other worlds that Julie told me about somehow more plausible. I also remember being alone in the bedroom after school, leafing through the books in the nightstand beside our bed, trying to read one of the stories Julie had told me. But for a long time, I saw only lines on a page. Next to riding Julie's two-wheeler, learning to read like her became my first conscious ambition in life.

During this period, when I was five, six, and seven years old, I didn't make the connection between newspapers or Julie's stories and learning to read and write in school, not deliberately anyway. Nor did I realize that newspapers, books, and stories came from real people. I certainly didn't know that I could make up my own story. Knowledge of this conspiracy among readers and writers could not be derived from the Dick and Jane basal reading series of the early sixties, my sole source of *official* information regarding things in print. The way I remember it is that reading at home meant reading for either information or pleasure, while school reading meant the sounds and shape of the alphabet. I don't recall considering writing as anything other than penmanship. I accepted the division between home and school reading and writing without question. Still, I was one of the lucky ones because I had Julie's stories, the newspaper, and eventually the public library.

By the time I finished college, I had come to realize that the unreal world of school reading and writing was a regrettable but unavoidable fact of formal education, which I observed repeated many times as my younger brothers and sisters went through the same system after me. In the meantime, I had learned a lot more about the need for all kinds of print in our personal lives, both the factual and the fictional. It was, of course, stories that still held sway over me, and I headed off for graduate school in English to study novels. I hadn't thought much about the autobiographical stories of our lives, though, until the time came for me to tell my eight-year-old brother, Matthew, whom I had spoiled since the day he was born, of my pending departure. He stopped me mid-sentence and asked, "But who will remember?" At first I was confused by the question, and then startled. It seemed to me that he was asking me who would remember *him*—that is, his *story*, his history. Even at only eight years old, he seemed to sense that knowledge of his past was integral to his future, and he wanted assurance of its preservation.

In due time, I switched from English to education studies, and inevitably I began to look at how children learn to read and write. It is important to note, however, that before I could truly understand anything about stories or reading and writing in the classroom, I had to learn to be a teacher. I naturally assumed that this entailed learning *what* to teach, including beginning reading and writing, but *what* to teach didn't prove useful or interesting enough in the end. I became a teacher only after I learned to listen and watch. I also had to learn to wonder—I mean truly wonder—in the absence of a common history, who each child was: why he or she said and did what he or she said and did—in the classroom, in the hallway, on the playground. Of course, it was all so spectacular, I couldn't help but wonder. My compensation was a bird's-eye view of human development unfolding. I was pleased, though not surprised, to find curiosity and laughter in such little children. In far too many, however, I also found more pain than a rational society is willing to imagine in its youngest members.

My first lesson in the relationship between the stories of the children in our classrooms and a beginning reading and writing curriculum was named David. David was an intensely shy four-year-old with honey-colored skin and watchful gray eyes, rimmed with lashes of unbelievable length. I didn't know anyone could be so beautiful. At first, David met my efforts with a determined, almost defiant silence. My co-teacher and I kept trying, but his participation in our teacher-planned activities remained minimal. It was easy to see that he preferred to be alone with his small cars in the block corner. I wondered: who was this little boy who maintains such a fierce, consistent distance from me? What didn't I know about him? The weeks went on, and then, one winter day, as I chased him across a snowy playground in a spontaneous game of tag, he turned, and exclaimed with a broad smile, "I *like* you!" It was a beginning: the teaching I was to care about began at that moment, and the hidden stories of the children in classrooms were revealed in that moment.

David was a pre-kindergartener. My next challenge (I believed) was to "get him ready" for kindergarten, which, traditionally, called for pre-reading and writing instruction. David wasn't interested. Then, for no particular reason other than his growing preoccupation with the issue of fairness in the use of classroom materials, I took to writing turn-taking lists for everything, ensuring him of when his turn would be with the blocks, the bicycles, and other favorite toys. He checked the lists constantly. Along the way he memorized the spelling of the other children's names, and made use of this information to enter into conversation with them. ("Robin, it's your turn on the bike. I'm next.") I was fascinated. The lists seemed to calm David, as if the world appeared more manageable somehow. As it turned out—and I do think it was a coincidence—David appeared to be learning a great deal about the formation of print and the meaning of the written word from these lists: "Teacher, *bicycle* and *tricycle* are almost the same." I had stumbled onto a way to make the curriculum meet the needs of an individual child and not the other way around.

Making more use of stories and David's own story in particular would have been an even better activity for connecting basic reading and writing activities with his personal needs, but I hadn't discovered this method yet. When I finally did, the children's great joy in storytelling reminded me again and again of my brother Matthew's question from long ago—Who will remember?—and of his childish desire to be remembered—*to be known*. Now I take it for granted that if we allow them, young children will tell us their stories willingly, even desperately at times: they really do want us to know who they are. In a sense, they are both reporters *and* storytellers, for nothing more accurately reflects their thoughts than the stories they tell, though it is not always a real world they tell about.

As a parent, I have seen my own children pore over baby pictures in search of their past, which they can feel but barely remember, some evidence of their impact on the world. But by far their favorite moments occur when I tell them about when they were babies. Any supporting evidence from their baby books is another precious gift.

Many years and hundreds and hundreds of children's stories later, I am convinced that a successful beginning reading and writing curriculum simply cannot be divorced from the real lives of families, brothers and sisters, parents and children, teachers and students. Above all, teachers need to know who the children are in their classrooms: they need to know the children's stories. This is what "ought to be interesting" to teachers of young children. This book is an attempt to explore the place of stories in the real lives of children and in the real classrooms of pre-schools, elementary schools, daycare centers, and the home.

A Note to the Reader

At any point, the reader might want to take a look at appendix A, which contains samples of stories that children dictated to their teachers, and appendix B, which presents sample transcripts of tape recordings of typical dictation sessions.

Chapter One

❊

STORIES IN SEARCH OF CLASSROOMS

We are faced now with something of a puzzle. In the first years at school all appears to go very well. . . . However, when we consider what has happened by the time the children reach adolescence, we are forced to recognize that the promise of the early years frequently remains unfulfilled. . . . The problem then is to understand how something that begins so well can often end so badly . . . whether schooling really does begin as well as it seems to do or whether the brightness of the early years carries within itself the shadow of the darkness that is to come.

—Margaret Donaldson, *Children's Minds*

In the fall of 1991, I visited Kay Miller's fifth grade classroom as part of the Classroom Storytelling Project, a school partnership program in the Teachers' Network for Early Literacy in the Center for Education at Rice University. On both of the first two visits I read the children a story. When I finished, I asked for volunteers to play the different characters. We immediately acted out the story. The kids who didn't have parts were designated as the audience, though I occasionally enlisted their help in certain scenes, such as the barnyard cackle in *Could Be Worse* or the townspeople's cries in *The Five Chinese Brothers*. These classroom dramas resembled a mime production with narration—I read the story aloud and the actors enacted the various scenes. Occasionally the actors interrupted my reading to repeat dialogue. Sometimes I interrupted them to press for more interpretive action. "C'mon," I urged as I read from *The Five Chinese*

Brothers, "let's see what you'd *really* look like if you were holding the *whole* sea in your mouth."

On my third visit, Ms. Miller explained to the class that two kids would have a chance to tell me their own stories that day, and that I would write them down. She carefully explained to them that these stories, like the books I had read, would then be acted out. Later on, she told them, she would take over the story activities and I would come just to watch.

The two main goals of the Classroom Storytelling Project are to foster, first, the children's knowledge of stories in general, and second, their interest in writing their own stories. These goals unite in the children's development as both readers and writers. Although these goals may sound somewhat abstract and sterile, the classrooms in which we work are rarely so. Storytelling seems to work best in active, vibrant rooms, where teachers are curious about children, and children are permitted to be curious about learning. Our methods are relatively simple. A mentor teacher is paired with a resident teacher for the school year. Each week the mentor visits the resident teacher's classroom to observe the children telling and dramatizing stories. The children also participate in other literacy activities, such as journal writing, News of the Day (or Kid News), and so forth. Following each observation period, the mentor and resident teacher get together to discuss what they've seen that day. They look for what was interesting in the children's responses, and for ways the teacher might do better.

I had been introduced to the use of dictation and dramatization activities as a kindergarten teacher in Chicago by Gillian McNamee of the Erikson Institute. It was Vivian Paley of the University of Chicago Laboratory Schools who first discussed these activities in her book *Wally's Stories*. Through her unique ability to analyze seemingly minor classroom events and conversations, Paley wrote of how the children's stories and dramas contributed to their play and social development. Ten years later, in *The Boy Who Would Be a Helicopter*, she showed how the stories helped her to understand the development of a particularly troubled child. Paley's insights into the children's use of stories and dramas in the classroom provide a solid foundation for their additional success as reading and writing activities. It is precisely because of this broad-based appeal that they work so well towards more academic goals.

On this particular fall day in Ms. Miller's class, Jermaine seemed both eager and hesitant to be the first storyteller. He finally agreed, but only after Ms. Miller assured him that he could tell about anything he liked. His head went up. "Anything?" he pressed, eyebrows arched. "Anything," she said. By the shine in his dark eyes, I sensed there was a memory in need of telling.

We sat at a table with three other boys who were reading and talking, but mostly talking. He turned his back to them and began: "When I was four or five. . . ."

I wrote that down. He stopped.

"I went into a store and. . . ." He looked around and then up at me.

"Can I hold it?" he asked me.

"Excuse me?" I asked.

"Can I *hold* it?" He pointed to the pen.

"Do you mean my pen? Uh, sure," I said.

For a moment I wondered if this rough-and-tumble sort of guy, with large, now uncompromising eyes, had changed his mind about participating in storytelling. As I handed him the pen, however, he reached for the paper, too. After where I had written "When I was four or five years old," he very slowly wrote, "I stole some gum." He looked up at me again, with an inscrutable expression. Then he pushed the pen and paper back towards me, ready for me to continue writing.

"I couldn't say that part out loud," he whispered. There was a "you understand" tone in his voice. But thinking ahead to the story reading and drama that were to follow, I didn't understand. What difference did it make to Jermaine whether *he* said these words now, or *I* said them later? Granted, they revealed an apparently significant aspect of his story, but I still didn't understand why he wanted to write them himself. Suddenly I was reminded that, despite all my years in classrooms, I can still be confounded by what kids say and do.

"Jermaine," I whispered back, "do you understand that I am going to read this out loud, and you're supposed to *act this out*? And everyone will *see* you acting it out?"

"Yeah," he returned, extending the word into two syllables—another way of saying "I know, stupid." Despite his irritation, however, he gave me a second chance. "But I couldn't say it *out loud*. The other kids might *hear* me."

I was still confused. Jermaine couldn't let the other kids hear him say the words they would hear me read aloud as they watched him act them out. He was requesting both the right to privacy and a public confession. Was this his intention?

At first I couldn't say why Jermaine's behavior so threw me. It wasn't just that his words didn't make sense. Young children often present us with conundrums in telling their stories. "Once upon a time I was a Ninja

Turtle. And then I became a *real* Ninja Turtle," four-year-old Ryan dictated. "I was" a pretend character and then "I became" a "real" pretend character? Did Ryan mean to describe a dream-like sequence, where one first pretends to be a character, and then, in dream-like fantasy, one becomes that character? Perhaps he had seen some such drama on television or in a movie. At any rate, such limitations in language development sometimes create the appearance of egocentricity in young children: they seem unconcerned with making sense to the listener. I do not find this to be true. On the whole, I find that young children *intend* to be intelligible, though sometimes they are unable to coordinate their words with their thoughts, which is a very different state of mind than egocentrism. If we could understand their mental references and associations, we could see that most often they are being quite logical.

Jermaine's case, however, was complicated by the fact that he was older than most of the beginning storytellers we work with: he was eleven, a fifth grader. Even an immature fifth grader could be expected to grasp the contradiction in the situation. No, Jermaine's case was not one of simple language development. His problem—or rather, *my* problem— was not with what he was saying, but rather *how* he was saying it, or, more precisely, how he was *not* saying it. What did Jermaine stand to gain in not saying "out loud" the words "I stole some gum?" Wasn't it likely that the "other kids might hear" this story of petty thievery on the playground, in the restrooms, even in classroom whispers. Why not, then, in dictation?

Much later I came to realize that Jermaine had to write "I stole some gum" himself not only because these words constituted the very essence of the memory, the heart of his story, but because he suddenly realized he couldn't let me control these precious words. Nor could he share them with the boys at the table just yet. I realize now that those important words were written with Jermaine's most inner voice, which with time could become his *writer's* voice, given enough practice. Jermaine needed control of the pencil because anything less would mean giving up control of his story to me, to "school business." I suspect he was simply too smart to risk its reception by both me and his classmates.

As for the dramatization of his story, it's possible that, though Jermaine insisted he understood that I would read aloud what he wouldn't let me write down, he didn't fully grasp the nuances of the situation. I think it's possible that, as late as the fall of his fifth grade year, Jermaine said yes to *school* language where he thought a yes was called for, because he somehow felt he had no choice. In this sense, he was like the very young children we see just starting out in the pre-schools and kindergartens.

Writing down his story had never happened before, and it touched a nerve somehow. Dramatizing the story, however, was somehow a foregone conclusion because I had previously demonstrated my control over class dramas when we acted out *Could Be Worse* and *The Five Chinese Brothers*. I think it's possible Jermaine might have said yes to this without truly grasping either the choice or the contradiction, not because he wasn't smart, but because he was too well defended. How did Jermaine come to maintain this separation of voice, of his inner self from his school life, all these years? At what cost?

The dramatization of Jermaine's story came off without a hitch. For a moment, the children appeared a little shocked at his admission of stealing. They all but gasped, and looked at me and Ms. Miller for our reactions. When we failed to comment one way or the other, they returned to the drama, laughing. In the end, their applause told Jermaine, Ms. Miller, and me that they approved of his story. The grin on Jermaine's face told me he was satisfied. Almost at once, the rest of the class clamored for a chance to tell their own stories. With more experience and trust, they might align their inner voices with what could become their writers' voices. Surely, even at fifth grade there still might be time for both a personal and academic payoff.

Perhaps I should pause here and explain why a fifth grader would be asked to dictate a story at all, when some teachers and educators would argue that he should be writing on his own. The fact was that Jermaine, like most of his classmates, was well below grade level in writing skills. According to their teacher, only a very few seemed confident in their writing abilities, and most of them claimed to detest writing. Ms. Miller and I were gambling that dictation (which relieves the child of the pressure to write and think at the same time) followed by class dramatization of their stories (where their stories could be heard and validated) could be a new beginning for these kids.

Others might wonder if classroom events like this one warrant such minute review. I strongly believe they do. We are kidding ourselves if we think learning is solely a by-product of the curriculum. Children are motivated to learn, just like grown-ups, by the impact of a hundred tiny truths in each day: the expression in someone's eyes, the approving or disapproving tone of someone's voice, even the colors of their notebook covers or tennis shoes. Disequilibrium sets in easily in children if we are not alert, and many children will never even make it to the curriculum. How can we hope to affect children's learning if we fail to consider their motives?

In the course of the next couple of months, other kids dictated stories with substantially more revealing circumstances of their lives outside of school. The subjects often involved street violence and, in some instances, conveyed the kids' overwhelming fear of abandonment (June's was titled "The Day Ms. Miller Died"). Interestingly, there was little anger in these grim scenarios—though I can only suppose that adolescence would eventually bring that, too. For now, many of the stories even had a comic overtone, as if the children had learned to laugh in order to avoid crying.

My friend and colleague Marvin Hoffman insists that we must admit to the failures as well as the successes in our classroom efforts if we are to be of any use to our students. At first it looked as if the experiment in Ms. Miller's fifth grade class was a success. I was thrilled. Eventually, our efforts in the Classroom Storytelling Project proved unsuccessful in this fifth grade classroom for the simple reason that we were forced to discontinue it before the end of the semester. In fairness, there was no one to blame—no one we knew anyway. Ms. Miller was a teacher with intelligence and, most of all, with heart, a precious asset in her inner-city classroom. The principal was an innovative educator who had welcomed us into her building. Despite our initial success with the children, however, the Classroom Storytelling Project could not promise an immediate improvement in the class' test scores or "formula writing" abilities: Jermaine's breakthrough in sharing his story of petty thievery would do little to contribute to his success with the business of school and school writing, and storytelling was shelved in favor of test preparation. Many teachers find themselves in this bind. No teacher wants to see her children fail. When you live with children every day, you hunger for their success according to whatever measurement is forced upon them. You care too much to say it doesn't matter. The grim truth is that, even in the most supportive of schools, there is rarely time to know our children's stories, for no statistic can measure how knowing them is related to school business and school success.

Jermaine had made it all the way to fifth grade without bringing his real story to school. Many kids continue on through junior high school and high school in the same silence. When does the silencing of our children's voices begin?

❧ *Before Reading and Writing*

It seems that we know so much about young children, but often we fail to remember what is really important to them. We praise them mindlessly for minor accomplishments, and then forget that each birthday automatically makes them taller. We promise them "tomorrow," but mean never. We laugh at their games because we forget that the good guys must always win, for young egos, like young bodies, are vulnerable, and need protection. Our failure to remember the impact of the early childhood years becomes even more insidious when, in the mistaken belief that a broken spirit is the same as a cooperative spirit, we make young children dependent on *us* to know if they are good, or bad, or smart. Where is the future in that?

The awful truth is that we don't do right by all children just starting out in our schools and pre-schools. Sometimes it happens that they are so needy, and the resources so few. Or maybe they are so smart, and the curriculum so dumb. Sometimes it happens that they look and act quite differently than we do, and the distance between us becomes part of the relationship. It is not enough to say that our schools are underfinanced or that high-quality early childhood programs are too costly to provide each young child with the encouragement and tools to be successful in the upper grades. Money can fix a lot of ills in our nation's schools, make no mistake about it. But it can't remove the need for children to hide who they are; only teachers can do that. Nor can money fix a curriculum that does not encourage children to make use of their past experiences. Yet often we reward young children at the start of their intellectual lives for suspending their social and emotional—as well as their *thinking*—selves in favor of an artificial, materials-based, teacher-centered curriculum. Too often we reward young children for parroting back material far in advance of their ability to comprehend it, or far worse, material they have absolutely no interest in. How often do we suggest by word and deed that learning can be bought at the teachers' store and that it can happen in fifteen-minute blocks of time? Far too often. Although a cookie-cutter approach to early childhood education is decried by almost all of our nation's top educators and institutions, generally speaking it is the children who must adapt to our schools, not the other way around.

Almost eighty years ago John Dewey wrote, "There are three things about the old-fashioned school that must be changed if schools are to reflect modern society: first, the subject matter, second, the way the teacher handles it, and third, the way the pupils handle it."[1] Since then, there has been no end to the criticisms of our nation's schools. In a sense, we should never expect to be finished with the task of reforming our schools because, quite simply, the nation and its peoples change too fast for ultimate solutions. There will always be new questions about the human mind and how it works that will produce new educational agendas and calls for reform, just as there will always be teachers and schools going about doing it the wrong way, and more teachers and critics waiting to swoop down and make it better. This should not make us cynical about school reform efforts, but rather grateful for them.

Yet often, despite our best efforts, we just don't reach young children on the inside, where they hide their stories. We know it, and they know it. We know it by the stiffness of their shoulders as they turn away when we try to comfort them. We know it by the defiance in their eyes, or worse, by the glaze. We know it by the parrot-like "Yes, ma'am. No, ma'am." If eleven-year-olds like Jermaine can be so disaffected from school—the most potentially influential experience of their lives beyond the family—what about nine-year-olds, six-year-olds?

Try four-year-olds. Try Maura, rolled up in a ball, crying, in the housekeeping corner of her pre-kindergarten classroom. She had banged her ear and head on a table when she tripped in her play high heels. "What's the matter, Maura?" the teacher called. Maura looked up, startled. She quickly stifled her sobs, straightened out her little body, and went back to play, her face tear stained, her mouth tight. Even in obvious pain, she would not tell. The real tragedy in failing to reach even the youngest children in our care does not stem from the children, or their much publicized "lack of preparation" for school, or their "unreadiness to learn,"[2] but from our lack of response to their personal and developmental histories—in other words, *to who they are and how they think*. This means that each teacher must strive to know who the children are who have come to share their very lives with her. In every way possible, her classroom and curriculum must make room for each one of the children's stories, for only then will the children be free to trust teachers, and, thus, free to learn.

Stories—lots of stories, adult-authored and child-authored, stories in the service of creating a common classroom culture—can be a basic vehicle for individual development, for through stories young children can confront their personal and imaginative worlds so that they may come to understand them. To quote Jason Epstein, children need stories in their lives "for the sake of learning something, or more precisely, for the sake of becoming something—something more grownup than one had been

before."[3] In this sense, stories become the foundation of our children's emotional and intellectual education. This is the education most worth having when you are two or four or eight years old. As we approach the end of the century, we know more about young children's development than ever before. It would be irresponsible of us not to make use of this information to craft a curriculum that will respond to who they are and how they think. It is not only the most humane approach to education, it will, in the long run, prove the most effective.

🌿 *Language Development and Reading and Writing Instruction*

Teachers in the best early childhood programs view a young child's education as an exploration, an interaction with ideas and materials that make up the real world. Specific curricula almost always include (but are not limited to) blocks, water play, and art. Smart primary grade teachers have incorporated such hands-on activities into their classrooms, too. These are basic ways for young children to explore the physical, sensorial, and logical world, as they build the foundations of scientific and mathematical knowledge.

The foundation of language development is another matter, relying as it does on less concrete experiences. In textbook terms, language development can cover everything from learning to talk to learning to read and write. However, language development, and its school counterparts reading and writing, should not be merely a question of producing, decoding, and encoding language, but rather one of *knowing* language—as a fine carpenter knows his tools, as a mother knows her baby's face. Children who hear stories regularly will become intimate with language in this same way. Stories can be the concrete materials young children use to develop, expand, and increase their language skills, much the same way they use concrete materials when building their skills in other areas, such as science, math, and art.

Furthermore, child psychologist Margaret Donaldson argues that stories enhance children's language development, not because of their use of language per se, but because of their grounding in "human intentions."[4] Donaldson believes that even the very youngest children can recognize human intentions in stories, if they are based on some point or purpose that makes sense in life. To Donaldson, understanding language at this level eventually produces an awareness of and a control over language that is fundamental to the development of self-consciousness in thinking, a critical factor in the growth of intellect. Children's earliest education, therefore, should always include stories: the stories of our common heritage, such as folk tales, as well as children's own individual stories, giving them access to the human intentions from which, Donaldson says, all true learning must spring.

Coincidentally—and it is a stroke of great luck—an added incentive to saturating our children's lives with stories is the positive impact this has on the more academic tasks of learning to read and write. One cannot count the number of pages that have been devoted to the subject, the theory, the teaching, the remediation, etc. of children learning to read and write, and we still don't have it right: look at the nation's appalling illiteracy rate, or the fact that some so-called readers and writers have never read a book for pleasure or never written a letter. It's no wonder that teachers are no longer sure what accounts for a child's success in mastering reading and writing. The reading experts may think *they've* got it right. But even good teachers are humbled by those kids who don't get it at all, just as they are by those kids who get it *despite* the curriculum.

Literacy expert Frank Smith suggests that the problem lies in looking for the answer in the first place. "The only practical educational conclusion that can be drawn from an analysis of the relatively few fundamental ideas that have come, gone, and continually returned throughout over twenty centuries of reading instruction—always with the result that some children have learned to read but others have failed—is that the universal concern should change from what teachers should *do* to what teachers should *know*." What teachers should know, he argues, is that reading is a matter of being invited into what he calls the "literacy club" by an experienced, welcoming reader.⁵

It is important to recognize that Smith's invitation to the "literacy club" will not come by osmosis to the young child. Nor will it come on the final page of a basal reader. Teachers will need to play an active role by both modeling and nurturing a young child's personal relationship with stories and writing. For the sake of clarity, it is necessary to distinguish between the development of a child's "relationship to stories" (or "relationship to writing") and to what current reading theory calls "print awareness."⁶ "Print awareness" aptly describes the child's sensitivity to the presence and use of print in the environment. *Relationships* to both stories and writing extend this cognitive awareness of print to include an engagement of the heart as well as the mind. These two rather profound relationships begin as one in the child's earliest experiences with picture books, perhaps as an infant on a parent's lap, feeling cozy and protected while also intrigued by the bright pictures and the words that the grown-up reads. Eventually the relationship extends to writing in the environment at large: writing that the young child produces in an effort to imitate what he or she sees on paper. Young children are constantly developing and revising their ideas about print. They also become more and more aware that the grown-ups they love can read and write. Learning to read and write, then, is also a way of emulating these loved ones. This is the beginning of reading and writing. Only much later in the process can we talk about reading and writing instruction.

Besides my personal interest in stories and classroom writing, the most important contribution to my understanding of how young children develop the foundations of reading and writing has been the opportunity to observe my own children growing up, experimenting with reading and writing in informal, spontaneous, and purposeful play. Nancie Atwell, whose books and essays have contributed so much to the writing process movement, described her transition from middle school teacher to mother in her eloquent essay, "Bringing It All Back Home." Reversing this idea, I urge teachers of young children to consider "bringing it all from home," in order to understand how children become readers and writers in the first place. The first time I observed my oldest daughter, at around twelve months, turn an upside-down book right side up and assume a reader's expression, or the first time I heard her younger sister, at three and a half, remark about a story she had just told me, "My story's about a kitten, but it's *really* about me," I knew I was witnessing the process of becoming a reader and writer. These lessons from home have been well documented. What they tell us is that reading and writing are not by-products of formal learning, but the by-products of living in a real world where, as the title of John Holt's last book on reading and writing put it, children are *learning all the time.*

---

1. Dewey, John, *Schools of Tomorrow*, p. 170.
2. Boyer, Ernest, *Ready to Learn*, p. 135.
3. Epstein, Jason, "'Good Bunnies Must Always Obey,'" in Sheila Egoff's *Only Connect*, p. 84.
4. Donaldson, Margaret, *Children's Minds*, p. 127.
5. Smith, Frank, *Reading without Nonsense*, p. 124.
6. Sulzby, Elizabeth and Teale, William, *Emergent Literacy*, p. xvii.

Chapter Two

✿

LESSONS FROM HOME

Kyle was not yet four and her baby sister was only a few days old. I was read-ing That New Baby, *the story of another big sister's disappointment and frus-tration after the arrival of a new baby. Kyle became calm for the first time since I had come home from the hospital. When I finished, she grabbed the book and clutched it to her chest. "This," she whispered, "is going to be a wonderful book!"*

In 1978, the University of Chicago hosted a national Narrative Confer-ence at which scholars in literature, psychology, history, and other disciplines explored the historical role of narrative. The conference ended with fiction writer and poet Ursula K. Le Guin. The audience expected—and hoped—that she would read from one of her works. She startled and delighted the academic audience with a very brief speech, which began something like this: "It was a dark and stormy night, and an Indian guide sat beside the campfire, and he told this story: [long pause] 'It was a dark and stormy night, and an Indian guide sat beside the campfire, and. . . .'" It was very funny in such a serious conference.

More than a decade later, ten young children gathered in my living room for a Halloween party. After a costume parade, orange cupcakes, and dunking for apples, two of the eldest (both seven-year-olds) told a story in unison that one of them had learned on the school playground, and had taught her friend that very same day: "It was a dark and stormy night, and a gremlin sat beside the campfire, and he told this story: 'It was a dark and stormy night, and a gremlin sat around the campfire, and—'" The duo paused, and looked at the grown-ups with knowing half-smiles. Then they laughed heartily, sure of the joke. The other six- and seven-year-olds in the group laughed, too. Confounding social and cognitive expectations is a favorite activity with six- through nine-year-olds. The three-year-olds in the group, who didn't get the joke, laughed because the older ones did, pleased to be included in this big-kid event. The one-year-old walked in and out of the group, only just beginning his education in storytelling.

The place of stories in the history of culture has fascinated academics for a long time. As Le Guin reminded us, however, the stories themselves supersede our analysis of them. But for young children just entering the culture, the place of stories in their world is never an academic question. For children, stories always have something to do with life in the present; their purpose is to help young children answer questions about the world as they experience it now. These are the reasons that stories can slip so easily into the home environment, where, in contrast to schools, they are not confined to storytime or language arts. The simple fact is that, for most American children past the age of two, school learning is not the same as out-of-school learning. School learning is programmed, timed, and encapsulated, whereas out-of-school learning usually arises out of a meaningful and present context. Nowhere is this more clear than in the contrast between reading and writing in the home, in the form of stories and meaningful print, and reading and writing in school.

In the last few years, many educators have tried to bridge this gap between home and school literacy, as evidenced by the widespread interest in emerging literacy, the Whole Language and the writing process movements, and other approaches to reading and writing that rely on books and the children's own writing. In my view, however, stories for their own sake, by both adults and children, have yet to earn their rightful place at the center of this effort. Far too often, stories and story writing are used to measure what children know about academic subjects, rather than what they *might* know, or might like to know about the world. A friend of mine who works with teachers to improve children's writing described the following scenario. It seems that the second graders in a local school had recently taken a standardized test that, among other things, called upon them to write a story about forests. Most of the children—relatively poor, inner-city kids, miles if not hours from the nearest forest—did poorly on the test. "These children don't know anything," their teacher complained. "They've had no experiences." No experiences the teacher—or the test designers—could appreciate, anyway.

The historical reason for sending children to school in the first place was to teach them to read and write, but if we, as educators, could understand the subtle and social nature of a child's first experiences with reading and writing in the home, we would be less inclined to teach reading and writing only as an academic subject. For this reason, I'd like to take a closer look at some examples of home-style literacy development. I concentrate on toddlers because the interpersonal nature of reading and writing development is so very explicit during this age, and because children who lack this foundation in reading and writing often have the most difficulty learning to read and write in our classrooms. This is not to say, however, that our classrooms can't replicate these experiences.

❦ *A Relationship to Stories in the Home*

Goodnight Moon by Margaret Wise Brown is a simple picture book. The title says it all. "Goodnight moon. Goodnight bears. Goodnight chairs. . . . Goodnight noises everywhere." Sometime around nine months, most babies take to this book like a new and favorite food. Some parents report that by the time their children are two years old, they have heard the story over two hundred times. Why? They can't read it. Few have probably seen a bear. The pictures, somewhat dark and old-fashioned, represent a room that is probably very different than their own. Why do they love it so, almost fifty years after it was first published?

First of all, consider the social and personal context of hearing the story, from the infant's point of view. Nine-month-olds, of course, don't sit on the floor to hear a story, they sit in your lap. A mother's or father's lap is cozy. The story is most often read after dinner and the evening bath, and before bedtime. Baby is fed, clean, and comfortable. Going to sleep can be a routine that babies look forward to because it often brings mother's or father's attention, as well as the somatic pleasure in feeling sleepy. Life, however, isn't this simple. Around nine months or so, going to bed also can raise some fretful feelings in babies, as they become more and more conscious of their actual separateness from mother and father. No wonder elaborate routines spring up in families around the bedtime hour. Saying goodnight takes on greater and greater significance and feeling for the infant. He or she is ripe for some extension of these feelings. A story can be that extension: the text of *Goodnight Moon* plays out a real-life scenario, and even improves on it, by practicing the separation over and over again, intentionally, with loving words, and a sweet, unrushed rhythm.

Goodnight Moon's primary appeal is not literary, but developmental—at this point, the baby doesn't care if it's a book or not. Given the opportunity, however, the baby will look to other books to satisfy him or her as *Goodnight Moon* did. Simple naming or sound books such as *Babies*, *I Am a Baby Dinosaur*, and *Baby Ben's Bow Wow Book* are other favorites. The moment of true engagement with books comes when the baby becomes conscious, at least on some primitive level, that books can reflect his or her own life. My daughter Jess' experience as a twelve-month-old with *Pat the Bunny*, another classic, offers a good example. I had been reading the book to her, by popular demand, for a week or so, playfully acting out the text as I read, patting the bunny, smelling the flowers, etc. Then, on about the tenth go-round, when we got to the picture of the father shaving his scratchy beard, she wriggled out of my lap. She walked through the house until she found her own father, and she gestured for him to bend down, which he did. At this, she stroked his chin, and promptly returned to me to finish the story. For several weeks after that, this scene was repeated without fail. Indeed, Jess' urge to reenact the book was almost irrepressible. Eventually, she seemed to accept the fact that she could remember her father's beard without touching it, and was content to stroke only the illustration. In a sense, Jess had learned that her life was not the same as the story. She could identify with the story, but she could also separate herself from it. This is an important first step in a child's relationship to books.

As toddlers grow older, it is not uncommon to hear them consciously reflect on the illustrations in picture books. Books, they are discovering, can be about many things that are of general interest to them. Whereas at a year younger Jess had to demonstrate what she knew about a book through action, two- and three-year-olds simply say it, through declarations of ownership, as teachers read aloud. "*I* have a baby" or "*I* have a boat" or "My mommy has a red car." Toddlers also imitate each other's declarations of ownership, repeating—true or not—the assertions of friends. There is no need to challenge these assertions. "You do?" or "Okay" is an appropriate response, because sharing grows out of owning, an important developmental issue for this age group, and the child is merely trying on some new possibilities. Again, the literary value of the book is not primary. Personal connections drive the child's interest.

Before a school meeting one evening, I heard parents of three- and four-year-olds discussing their children's favorite books. Parents, who I suspected read regularly to their children, reported that as the children grew out of infancy and chose their own books to be read, the books acquired a definite lifespan, some lasting as long as six months to a year. The group was laughing, because kids' reading habits and tastes were funny to them. The parents took stabs at why some books appealed more

than others. One little boy wanted the same one over and over, for security's sake, said his mother. Another little guy wanted only books with machines in them. "Perpetuating gender stereotypes," his mother explained with a sigh. In one home, *Sleeping Beauty* was the only choice for bedtime reading. It was a princess phase. Another sigh. Other books didn't even make it to a second reading regardless of the wonderful illustrations or lavishness of the book.

What struck me about the parents' descriptions of their children's reading choices was the parents' willingness to be led by their children's personal pursuit of stories. It wasn't just that they knew reading in the early childhood years was a factor in school success. They seemed to take pleasure in the fact that children pursued their favorite stories for some inherent, basic developmental need. In contrast, parents who see their children's relationship to books merely as a measure of later academic success are often anxious that their children be taught to read as soon as possible. This type of parent usually meets resistance from their children, however, and almost always from their children's pre-school teachers, who wish parents would stick to parenting and let teachers do the teaching. But teachers should emulate parents such as those at our school meeting that night. Children who have been read to at home for the pleasure of it, and who, in addition, have writing materials at their disposal (paper, crayons, pencils), usually arrive in our pre-schools with very positive feelings about books and stories. On average, they learn to read easily in due time. This should be more than a directional sign for us as educators of young children, it should be a warning sign.

Another significant difference between stories in school and stories in the home is the way in which children's play at home will often contain elements from their favorite books. "Who's that tripping over my bridge?" roared a three-year-old, whose favorite book at the moment was *The Three Billy Goats Gruff*, as he played with small plastic people-like figures on the living room rug. He had one figure hiding under the lid of his Lego container, while he tramped the other across it. Parents tend to support this kind of play through their approval of it, though rarely systematically. Pre-schools don't actively discourage book-related play, nor do they cultivate it, which would be simple to do in the classroom. Dramatization of books, which I discuss in chapter four, is one sure way to do it. Another way is the creation of story baskets, which were first shown to me by Houston teacher Mary-o Yeager. She was always on the lookout for any cheap commercial figures that either represented book characters or could substitute for them. Small plastic figures of the cast of *Snow White*, for example, can be found in many toy stores, teachers' catalogues, or at Disneyland and Disney World, of course. After reading the book to the children, Ms. Yeager simply put the figures in a basket with the book and, displayed it prominently in the room where it can be played with during appropriate times. Figures for *The Three Little Pigs, The Three Bears,* and *The Three Billy Goats Gruff* are easy to find in any farm or zoo collection.

❦ Using Stories on Video

Another way that stories can spill over into children's life at home is through the judicious use of videos. When I was in high school, my friends and I worried that seeing *Gone with the Wind* on film might "ruin the book." How wrong we were. Likewise, my experience has been that a child who loves the *Madeline* or *Babar* books will love them even more after seeing the movie. (Madeline and Babar stuffed dolls are also available, along with other popular picture book characters, such as Max from *Where the Wild Things Are*.)

Any parent with a VCR can take advantage of the video explosion to stimulate a child's interest in books. Since the film version of a book is rarely the same as the book itself, experiencing both of them offers lots of opportunities for parent and child to talk about what amounts to literary ownership. By contrasting the book and the movie, if only in terms of which one they liked better, even very young children can see that stories and books can be changed for better or worse. This in turn helps them to become more critical readers and viewers in the future, as well as to assume more control over their own writing. A further advantage of videos is that a film version of a book or story can make a more difficult piece more accessible for a child, either before a parent reads it or before the child attempts to read it alone. *The Chronicles of Narnia,* for example, became a popular read-aloud book with some first grade children and parents only after the PBS version was aired. Prior knowledge of how the plot unfolds, as well as visual images of Narnia and the odd cast of characters, gave these young listeners the patience to wade through the book's rather detailed descriptions when it was read to them.

Sometimes literary success through videos comes quite unintentionally. One Friday evening, on a whim, I decided to rent Shirley Temple's *Heidi,* one of my favorite movies from childhood. My four-and-a-half-year-old daughter Kyle and I cried our way through the story of the Swiss orphan who was kidnapped from her home in the Alps, subjected to the cruelty of the awful Fraulein Rottenmeir, and finally reunited with her grandfather. Despite Kyle's obvious enjoyment of the movie, I was surprised when in the ensuing weeks *Heidi* became one of the "stories" she asked me to retell over and over, even though we had not read the book yet. Kyle's fascination with the Heidi story continued for a couple of months. My husband and I would find her tending to the "goats" (a stuffed dog and bear), or acting out other parts of the story, or running from room to room yelling, "Grandfather, Grandfather, where are you Grandfather?" She had a corduroy skirt and vest with a Swiss look about it that became the outfit of choice. Next, she began to pick up the nearest available book and pretend it was *Heidi*, and proceed to "read" it aloud to herself.

At this point I offered to read her the original story by Johanna Spyri. Thus far I had avoided it, fearing the old-fashioned style and vocabulary were too advanced for a child under five. But these were learning-to-read issues, and by then I had a mother's goal: to provide another way to extend Kyle's deeply satisfying play in whatever way possible. So, lacking mountains and goatherds, I resorted to the book. I counted on Kyle to tell me, either by word or action, if it was too hard for her. In fact the book is far too difficult for a pre-schooler's comprehension, yet night after night Kyle begged me to read just one more chapter. I was fairly certain that most of it was over her head, but her memory of the basic story line (from the movie version) seemed to carry her through the lengthy descriptions of nature and Spyri's philosophical musings.

During the two weeks it took me to read the book aloud, Kyle's role as a listener to stories began to blossom into that of a reader of stories. She now began to insist that I run my finger under the words as I read aloud. She also started to interrupt my reading, something she had never done before, to ask where I was on the page. She would then look intently at the words, as if to discover something. Up to this point, she had never demonstrated any particular knowledge of print. Unlike most of her four-year-old friends, she had not been taught to write her name, nor did she show a lot of interest in the alphabet in general, though she loved to draw. Suddenly, towards the end of the book, she began to ask me to teach her to read. She moaned about all the books she couldn't read, especially *Heidi*. I told her that teaching children to read wasn't my job, but that she would learn in due time. Then one afternoon when we were almost at the end of the book, she stood on the bed, put her hands on her hips, and asked firmly, "WHEN are you going to teach me to read?" She was furious with me.

Vygotsky wrote that "the teaching of reading and writing must be organized in such a way that it becomes necessary for something."[1] Necessary in the children's lives, not the parents' or the teachers'. The story of Kyle and *Heidi* is a good example of a child's becoming invested in print, in what the words say, in what the story reveals to her about people—Donaldson's "human intentions"—and the world they inhabit. This is what stories can do. What proved to be a pivotal experience in Kyle's life (she started reading on her own soon afterwards) began with an old movie on video. There are lots of wonderful old movies based on children's classics that parents indulge in because these films feel good, or because they bring back pleasant memories of childhood, or because they're simply great stories. Children can sense their parents' positive attitude as they watch these movies. Invariably, if the books themselves are available afterwards, children's curiosity will be aroused, and they will open them.

A Relationship to Print in the Home

There are many ways that parents introduce young children to print in the environment—their own names, street signs, stop signs, business signs, price tags, and so on. Young children at home also observe parents actively engaged in meaningful writing activities, such as composing a grocery list, looking up a telephone number, or sending a get-well card. Sometimes it's an older sibling that will stimulate a younger one's interest in print by just doing homework or checking the baseball scores. It is obvious that a large part of children's experience with print and writing in the home arises naturally out of everyday situations. Writing, like reading, is a part of everyday life, despite the fact that schools have treated it like a special event or a visiting cousin for so long.

When parents don't try to teach their children about reading and writing, they are often surprised by their young children's knowledge of print. As in many areas of development that have academic counterparts, it is hard to believe that learning can occur so indirectly. I had an experience like this in the midst of a Saturday morning breakfast with my daughter Jess, then two and a half. I was putting the milk away and she was sitting at the kitchen table, her back to me, eating a bowl of cereal. I noticed that she pulled the cereal box closer as she ate. I smiled, for here was a clear attempt to imitate her older sister, who recently had become an avid cereal box reader. My reaction is typical of many parents. We take great pleasure in observing a younger sibling imitating an older one. In any case,

I was quite amused when Jess interrupted her eating and asked, "Mommy, what does *B R X D* say?" She was pointing to the picture on the back of the box. Her sister would often ask a similar question, though she, being a reader at the time, would be calling out not just any letters, as Jess had done, but the actual letters on the box. This little one, however, did not know the correct names of the letters. My guess is that she wasn't even aware that particular letters had particular shapes. What is more important here is her nascent awareness that the letters *said something,* that they *added up to something besides themselves.* "Hmmm," I paused, searching for an answer that would make sense to her without disrupting her image of herself acting as her sister acted. Finally I answered, "It says, 'A boy on a bicycle.'" That was the picture on the box, so I assumed that would satisfy her.

She accepted my answer without comment, and then she ran her finger over the picture of the boy on the bicycle. "Mommy, what does 'bicycle' say?" *B R X D.* Bicycle. What I thought was only an exercise in hero worship was also a very important exercise in early literacy development for Jess. Her question about the bicycle, however, showed me that she hadn't yet realized that while letters stood for something else, pictures stood for themselves, in other words, they "say" what they are. In terms of early literacy development, she was exploring the function of print before she had been taught its form.

Finally, it's important to keep in mind that Jess had borrowed the idea of reading the cereal box from her big sister. Jess' experience is a good illustration of the theory that learning to read and write is a social, not an isolated, experience, rooted in the examples, models, and demonstrations that young children are exposed to and practice in their everyday world at home.

❄ *The School Connection*

Goodnight Moon, Pat the Bunny, Heidi, and cereal boxes are all lessons from home, but in order to benefit from them, strictly speaking, children have to *be* home. The fact is that children simply spend less time in the home nowadays as a result of the tremendous rise in the number of working parents. To think that schools, daycare centers, and extended-day programs will be an exact substitute for the home environment is unreasonable. This does not obviate the need for teachers to create rich and yet natural literacy environments that encourage the intimate and yet practical use of reading and writing materials similar to those found in the home. The need has never been greater. There is no reason that schools and daycare centers cannot make use of the knowledge that children seem to learn to read and write best in environments in which personal and social needs dictate their pursuits.

Trinity School for Young Children in Houston, Texas, is one example of an all-day program for children ages eighteen months through the pre-kindergarten year that devoted special attention to the foundations of reading and writing. Trinity teachers made no attempt to teach children to read, but instead tried to create classrooms where reading and writing seemed to arise naturally out of the business of the day and the needs of the kids. First they made sure each class library was well stocked (and that books rotated on a regular basis). The local library and the paperback book clubs such as Scholastic made this relatively inexpensive. Second, regardless of the age of the children, they made sure that every classroom had plenty of the story baskets I mentioned earlier. Third, they made writing materials available at all times in the Writing Center or other appropriate areas.

Next the teachers took a careful look at the schedule. While each class had a morning story time, stories were also read aloud before nap, after nap, before going home, and throughout the day. Individual story time was also stressed, for it is important that beginning readers and writers have a chance to sit on a grown-up's lap, or lean against her when reading, which is not feasible during the formal group story time. As a result, school children associate greater warmth and security with books, and feel freer to ask questions about the pictures and text, just like children at home. Once story times were established, the teachers scheduled regular opportunities for the children to dramatize adult-authored stories, as well as to dictate and dramatize their own stories.

It wasn't uncommon for each class to have a particular favorite that seemed to pervade their play and their own storytelling for months on end, although the teachers could never predict which story would capture the group's imagination. For two years running, Ms. Yeager's two- and three-year-old class seemed obsessed with *The Wizard of Oz*. It began innocently enough when Ms. Yeager brought in the MGM soundtrack and played it frequently during free play. Who would have guessed that the sound of Miss Gulch's arrival and the oncoming twister would make two- and three-year-olds stop their play and listen? Children who arrived very early, between 7 and 8 A.M., asked for the record to be played as soon as they arrived. (Children in daycare often look for these reminders of yesterday first thing in the morning.) Children who arrived later were greeted with the record's familiar sound.

Ms. Yeager responded to the children's interest in the record by providing the original book, as well as simplified versions of the story. She also brought in makeshift costumes, figurines, puppets, and other paraphernalia representing the book and movie. The children were delighted by these and other small items, such as a miniature egg timer (from the scene in which the hourglass measures Dorothy's imprisonment in the witch's castle).

In Mrs. Grant's class, it was *The Nutcracker* that became a long-standing theme after the kids became intrigued with the story behind the Tchaikovsky music, which their teacher chanced to play during clean-up time. A nutcracker-turned-prince, a mouse king, and, best of all, a little girl who throws her slipper at the mouse king proved to be an irresistible combination for these three- and four-year-olds. There are many, many versions of E. T. A. Hoffman's original book, making it easy for the teacher to find one that suited the kids best. The children were quite annoyed, however, to discover that in some versions the main character is called Klara, while in others she is Marie. They voted on Klara as the official choice for all the books, and would get agitated with their teacher when she forgot. Homemade costumes were again very popular during free play, as were cheap nutcrackers and plastic figurines. At the end of the day, it was not unusual for mothers and fathers to have to extract their little ones from the evening march of Klara and the wooden soldiers. When the children in these two classrooms had the opportunity to dictate their own stories, it was not surprising that many of them retold certain scenes or moments from *The Wizard of Oz* or *The Nutcracker.*

The teachers promoted the children's interest in both *The Wizard of Oz* and *The Nutcracker* for many reasons, not the least of which was because the children seemed interested in extending their play around them. In short, they let the children set the literary agenda of the classroom, much as parents do in the home. In contrast to parents, however, the teachers made overt efforts to extend the children's learning by linking their favorite stories to drama and dramatic play, to storytelling and writing.

🐾 Writing and Communication in the Classroom

At home, one of the first steps children take in becoming readers and writers is to develop expectations of print: first, that print can be read and written by adults or older siblings; and second, that they too will be readers and writers someday.[2] These expectations are usually cultivated as a by-product of listening to stories and reading and writing in the course of everyday life. Some children, of course, do not develop expectations of print in the home. Teachers of pre-schoolers, kindergarteners, and first and second graders who have not developed expectations of print at home should create as many opportunities to hear stories and simple messages as possible. On average, however, expectations of print begin relatively early, although evidence of this is sometimes fairly subtle.

Billy was a little boy at Trinity who showed developing expectations of print at about two years old. One day he was sitting on his cot, holding his favorite book, Anne Rockwell's *Trucks*, waiting for his teacher to read him a book before nap time (like the bedtime story at home). She was sitting with a little girl on the cot across from his. Billy was sort of bouncing in place and waving the beloved book. He became so impatient that he decided to take the matter into his own hands. "Teacher, *can* you read me this book?" His teacher heard him, but was somewhat distracted by the little girl, who she thought might be getting sick. "I don't know," she answered distractedly. The incredulity in Billy's voice was not to be missed when he asked, "You don't *know the words?*"

Billy's misinterpretation of his teacher's response reveals his expectation that adults will "know the words" in a picture book. By the age of two, Billy's experience had taught him that adults don't always stop their adult activities to play with small cars or get out the playdough, but the chances for their attention increase if a book is involved. I remember my eldest daughter once sighing and saying, "No one ever reads to me any more." It wasn't true, of course, but it produced the desired effect. Toddlers have also been known to use books as a means of gathering friends together ("Come on, guys, Mrs. Simmons is going to read the fire truck book"). Or they may use the situation to garner some one-on-one attention ("No, I don't want Melissa to listen, just me").

Expectations of print usually begin with stories because stories are so appealing to young children. Teachers of young children also should be alert for opportunities to write down something meaningful and personal for the children. This is not as simple as it sounds. After all, spontaneous writing at home arises directly out of an adult's need. Rarely do teachers have a need for writing in the classroom. As Judith Schickendanz points out, teachers of young children tend to concentrate on the children, who, since they can't read, require no written communication.[3] The natural tendency is to communicate only in the way they can understand: verbally. Limiting communication in the classroom to the spoken word, however, does not provide children with the model of writing that they get at home. In an unusual twist on the home environment, then, teachers can write down what they think is important to the child, who, although a non-reader, will come to value the written word as something with meaning for him or her.

Daniel was a Vietnamese child who, at approximately two years old, spoke no English. His mother told the teachers at Trinity School that he spoke only a little Vietnamese. Still, he jabbered constantly to his teachers and classmates, and appeared to understand quite a lot of what the teachers and other children said or asked. Soon after his second birthday, his mother had a new baby. His teacher posted a sign on the classroom door at Daniel's eye level that said, "Daniel has a new baby brother named Simon," which she read aloud to him. As the other children arrived that morning, she pointed to the sign, and read the news. Throughout the day, when a visitor or staff member came to the room, Daniel rushed up and pointed to the sign. He then tapped the sign repeatedly with his index finger and began to "talk" very fast. Every so often his teacher could distinguish a sound that closely resembled "baby," sort of like "baaab." At the end of the day, when parents arrived to pick up their children, Daniel again rushed up and tapped the sign. At one point, he went around to all the other signs in the room, which held messages such as "Ms. Allen has gone on a trip," tapping them, too, and saying the same word, "baaab." Daniel's apparent understanding that the written word can have particular and personal meaning is an important milestone in early literacy development.

❦ Stories for a Child at Risk

It is well known that the process of developing expectations of print does not come automatically to all children. We can speculate why, and find blame somewhere, but sooner or later these children arrive in a classroom. The sooner the better. The experience of Douglas, a young toddler, is a good illustration of how two teachers helped a child establish the basic foundations of early literacy in the classroom, using techniques from home. His story is worth recounting because Douglas was the type of child that makes teachers' jobs harder. He came to school (his first group experience) at nineteen months, a lovable child, but with a much shorter attention span than other children his age and almost no capacity to sit still, two attributes hardly conducive to listening to stories. Also, Douglas did not talk at all, which was not too unusual for a nineteen-month-old, but it was not clear he understood what was said to him either, which was unusual. By usual standards, Douglas was a child "at risk" in terms of future success in school.

As Douglas's teachers got to know him better in his first few weeks at school, they observed that his relationship to stories, let alone to books and print, was nonexistent. Early on, he was observed standing in the classroom, a long board book in his left hand, dangling open. He swung it slowly like a baseball bat, and then he let it drop to the floor. He ignored it and walked away. His teachers reported that he was not at all interested in listening to stories, alone or in a group. They said he did not seem to distinguish between books and other toys, except possibly to treat books as objects decidedly less interesting than others.

His mother confirmed his teachers' observation that Douglas was unaware of the value of books, or even of how they are supposed to be held. She said that she was waiting for him to develop an interest in books, and asked the teachers for help. Douglas's teachers did not wait for him to develop an interest in books. They created a small library for him that, despite his age and size, consisted of an assortment of books generally used with children younger than he: books with single pictures, pictures of babies, and baby items. They also read him various pop-up books, several of which required the reader to look for hidden objects. The teachers were not surprised to find that Douglas especially liked the peek-a-boo books. Douglas clearly was perplexed by his mother's all-day absence, and these books appeal to children just coming to grips with feelings of separation from their parents. With Douglas, the teachers' idea was to use books whose main appeal lies in the relationship between adult and child and whose basic themes deal with the naming of objects and with issues of separation.

Over the course of the next few months, with the teachers' steady help, Douglas began to develop an appreciation for books and for being read to one-on-one. A children's classic, *Frog Went A-Courtin,* became his absolute favorite. He learned to say some of the words that went with the pictures, even acting out "banjo on his knee" whenever that page came. His teachers learned that they could sing the first verse ("Over in the meadow, in the sand, in the sun, / Lived an old mother turtle and her little turtle one") when he was having difficulty at other times of the day and it would soothe him. Eventually, Douglas, who previously had demonstrated no interest in writing or drawing, began to do some rudimentary drawings of animals in the story.

Despite Douglas's tremendous progress in language and literacy development over the course of that year, he appeared indifferent to the fact that the other children in his class told—or dictated—stories to the teachers. He was equally uninterested in dramatization. Then, in May, Douglas volunteered to tell his first story. Taking his place beside the teacher, he watched as she wrote down what he told her.

Douglas's Story   *May 29*

Max!
Right there.
Melissa.
Douglas!

What followed next was one of those moments in teaching when the hard work finally pays off. As the teacher wrote down what Douglas was telling her, she echoed his words: "Melissa. Douglas!" She noted that, as she wrote and echoed his name, he patted his own chest. A quiet moment of victory, but victory nonetheless.

Douglas's second story, a month later, shows a greater manipulation of language:

Douglas's Story   *June 27*

Dinosaurs
Roar!!!
Dinosaur mommy saying, "Roar!"
Dinosaur baby saying, "Roar!"
Eating.

The End.

Although it is obvious that Douglas's first two stories are hardly stories in the sense of true narratives, his behavior as a "storyteller," demonstrates a burgeoning understanding that what can be said can be written down. When Douglas started his second year in school, at two and a half, his mood and affect during literacy activities were much more appropriate for his age. It was clear that he was on his way to joining the "literacy club." The important thing is that Douglas was still a toddler when he entered school for the first time. Many kindergarten teachers report that children as old as five and six are entering elementary schools with no relationship to stories, writing, and print whatsoever. The job facing these kindergarten teachers is not an impossible one, but certainly an unnecessary one, one that could easily have been avoided by a pre-school education like Douglas's, rich in stories and writing. These are lessons for teachers to borrow from home.

---

1. Vygotsky, Lev S., *Mind in Society*, p. 117.
2. See Holdaway, Don, *The Foundations of Literacy*.
3. Schickendanz, Judith, "Mom, What Does U-F-F Spell?" in *Language Arts*, vol. 61, no. 1 (1984), p. 12.

Chapter Three

✻

What I Had to Learn about Stories in Classrooms

She kept too much in herself, her life was such she had to keep too much in herself. My wisdom came too late.

—Tillie Olsen, *Tell Me A Riddle*

In the late seventies, when I began teaching kindergarten, I worried a great deal about tomorrow. My goal was to ensure that the children would be "ready" for first grade by June. The question that worried me the most was whether the first grade teacher would expect them, or most of them, to be reading and writing. Yet this was hardly the question that interested me the most about teaching kindergarten. My real interests lay in storytelling and play. At the time, however, stories and play seemed to me to be incompatible with the brass tacks of learning to read and write. This was before I understood that a story-based curriculum could be a basic vehicle for learning to read and write, and before I learned to value reading and writing in the world young children inhabit, not some world in what was—to the children—the far-off future. I know I was not alone in my experience then, nor would I be today.

🌿 *Great Expectations and the Fallacy of Readiness*

In my first year as a kindergarten teacher, the classroom schedule was divided between the formal lessons reserved for reading, writing, and math, which took place at the classroom tables, and the children's choice: free play. The informal lessons of reading and writing consisted of reading at least one picture book, dramatic play, and music. In September, formal lessons began with activities that emphasized spatial relations, visual discrimination, tracking, and other traditional "pre-reading" activities. By Christmas, the children had progressed to phonetic lessons and worksheets. Writing was limited to copying the alphabet. First upper case, then lower case. All of these lessons took place in a mandatory Circle Time or mandatory Table Time. This procedure was followed by every kindergarten teacher I knew.

As I understood it then—and I did try to understand—*preparing* children to be readers and writers could occur in an informal, play-based environment, but *teaching* them required formal lessons. I was assuming, naively, of course, that you couldn't "teach" children what they couldn't see and touch. Also, I was assuming that any activity children approached with a playlike attitude couldn't have academic value.

When I started teaching kindergarten, readiness was a popular idea in reading and writing instruction. The notion is that teachers should wait to teach reading and writing until the child demonstrates an interest. It is an idea that, on the surface, seems to make a lot of sense. It is worth noting, however, that while the now time-honored "readiness approach" to reading and writing development aims to account for children's different maturation rates, in reality it has some severe limitations. Even today, it is often interpreted only as a measure of phonics-readiness. Children are deemed to be ready to learn to read and write only when they are ready to tackle skills and sub-skills. From a developmental point of view, this is ridiculous. Children are "ready" to learn to read and write from birth, just as they are "ready" to talk, walk, and ride a bicycle in the sense that they possess an innate drive to do so. A good early childhood program will foster the development of language, logical thinking, and motor proficiency at all levels, beginning with approximations that are welcomed as heartily as the real things. In other words, skills are the last thing children learn in the achievement of any developmental goal, not the first.

Another problem with a readiness approach is the difficulty of assessing readiness. What are the indicators? I've heard readiness defined as everything from knowledge of the alphabet to writing one's name to the ability to sit still for long periods of time. Like many new teachers, I couldn't help but wonder where the children learned these things if someone didn't teach them. Also, I've observed schools whose notion of readiness creates a hierarchy in which children who aren't assessed to be "ready" to learn are denied the opportunity to experiment with the type of work or "big kid" activities assigned to their more advanced peers. Common sense tells us that this has a negative impact on a child's self-confidence.

Stories are rarely mentioned in the readiness approach except insofar as it is advocated that teachers read to their children every day. In classrooms filled with many competing activities, worksheets, and drills, teachers don't always have time to read to their students.

The Back to Basics movement was also popular when I started teaching. It is similar to the typical readiness curriculum in that it too promotes phonics and skills as the foundation of a reading and writing curriculum. The distinguishing factor is the child's need to demonstrate mastery of each skill level before being promoted to the next. Some early (usually self-taught) readers in these classrooms are subjected to the absurd experience of having to sit through lesson after lesson on skills that will teach them to read, when clearly they already know how to do it. One mother told me that in the first grade her self-taught daughter was told to "stop reading altogether" so that she could be taught the basic skills that, presumably, she missed in learning on her own.

It's also true that alternative approaches to the teaching of reading and writing existed back then. Variations on the Language Experience Approach were popular—alongside the worksheets, that is. We talked about "print immersion," and labels were omnipresent: "door," "blocks," and "games" greeted us everywhere we turned. We wrote letters to the police officer, fire fighter, and anyone else who came to visit us; and I wrote down the children's responses to the request "Tell me about your picture" on the hundreds of drawings and paintings the kindergarteners produced over the year.

As much as I preferred the Language Experience activities, the Back to Basics approach, with its sure-fire emphasis on phonics, drill, worksheets, and testing scores, was hard to ignore. As a beginning teacher, I couldn't identify the feeling, but I think of it now as the "just in case" approach to selecting a curriculum. If there was no harm, perhaps the extra drill would help the children get an edge on first grade, I reasoned. I hear many teachers of pre-school and kindergarten children express the same quandary over the need for basics today. The buzz words may be different, but the tension is identical.

✿ Becoming a Teacher

Like most beginning teachers, I put many hours into my classroom and lesson plans. My colleagues laughed at my earnestness, and my director called me the most expensive teacher she ever had, insistent as I was on clean fresh paper and new markers. Reading and writing, I felt then (as I do today), are aesthetic experiences (I once overheard a writer say he first wanted to become a writer because he liked the way his script looked across the page). Ironically, I often used my precious time and resources to create nothing more than personalized worksheets. Perhaps I thought they'd be more palatable to the children.

If phonics and basic skills were alive and well when I started teaching, their reputed value far exceeded their actual appeal to young children— or teachers. Secretly I wondered, feeling sadly mutinous, if children and teachers weren't doomed to use only a tiny part of their brains in the learning or teaching of reading and writing. Shouldn't I warn the children? In spite of the energy I invested in making my reading and writing lessons attractive to them, and no matter how much I justified the endeavor as a necessary passage to real reading and to stories, I received little intellectual stimulation from my efforts. One reason was that teaching reading and writing to kindergarteners in this way didn't require me to respond: I merely needed to follow the teacher's manual or, better yet, the alphabet. Any pre-school teacher—or publishing house—knows that a whole year's lessons can be easily constructed from the twenty-six letters of the alphabet. There are the letter of the week lessons, the beginning sounds lessons, objects that begin with . . ., objects that end with. . . . Color the picture that sounds like. . . . Circle the one that is the same as. . . . As I've admitted, for some misguided notion of purity, I insisted on making my own worksheets and materials, but I could have bought commercial versions of the same things at any teacher store, just as you can today.

The second reason I was not stimulated by my own teaching was that the kids—whether rich or poor, black or white—responded to my lessons only with predictable answers or confused silence. I felt sorry for them. Years later, my four-and-a-half-year-old daughter summed up my feelings for me when, in response to a lesson in phonics, she quite seriously exclaimed with a sigh, "This is really *rather* boring." She paused. "I think I'll wait until I'm five—or six—or seven to read." In other words, let me forestall this painful chore as long as possible. I laughed, because by that time I was confident she would learn to read sooner or later. I knew that phonics was really only a small part of reading and writing education, and her early literacy development wouldn't suffer without it.

I hadn't laughed years earlier, however, when five-year-old Kenneth defied my efforts to make him write his letters, jumping up from the table each time I put the pencil in his hand. Instead, I told his parents that he might need to be retained in kindergarten until he was "ready to learn." I didn't laugh when I told Colin's mother, or De Juan's, or Richard's—all boys who couldn't sit still in Circle Time—that they weren't "learning." Not what I was attempting to teach them anyway; again, they weren't "ready."

What did I think when the children in my morning circle looked at me with their "Are we done yet?" faces as I made my way through daily reading and writing lessons, keeping them from their real interests: play and each other?[1] I wonder now what happened to Meredith or Maria or Arturo, children who would sit in their assigned seats, at their assigned tables, looking past their morning's worksheet to their classmates in the block corner or the housekeeping area. They looked trapped in an invisible net. "Finish your work," I'd coax, kneeling beside these slowpokes. I'd whisper my bribe into their ears, "Then you can go *play*." Remembering their speedier classmates' block replicas of O'Hare airport, which sometimes ran the length of the room, or the intense dramas in the housekeeping corner, which Carmen would direct in her best "I AM THE MOTHER" voice, I now know where the real learning was going on in that classroom.

❦ Writing

For all the children in my kindergarten class, learning to write meant nothing more than learning to print; an idea I did little to counteract. I didn't know yet that kindergarteners had something to say, even though they could not spell or even print fluently.

A typical day's writing lesson consisted of a ditto sheet with rows of pre-printed letters on the left-hand side, which the children would copy until they reached the right. Teachers and parents tend to overlook how painstakingly difficult it is for young children to control their pencils for long periods of time. For many of my children, a page of letters to copy was an overwhelming task, extending Table Time well into the desired free play period, and creating unhappy, deprived five-year-olds. Tom was no exception.

Tom turned five in the September of his kindergarten year. Although this was his second year in the same school and my co-teacher and I knew

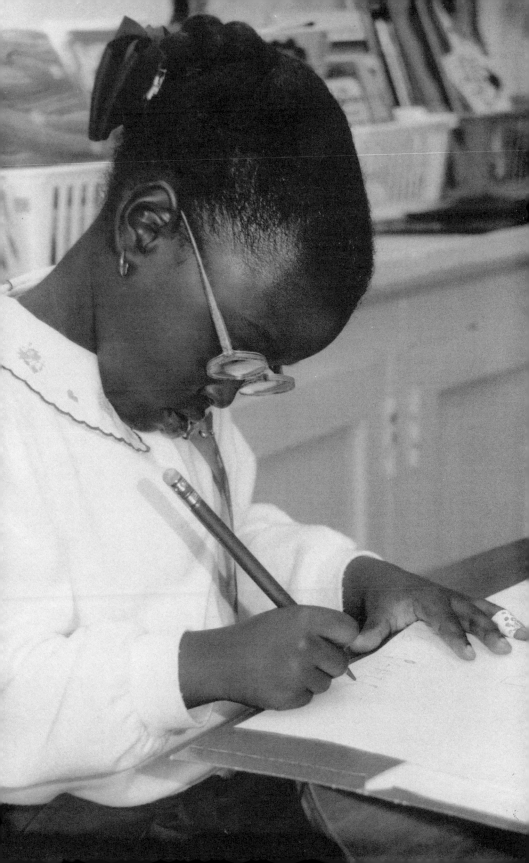

him well, he entered our kindergarten class reluctantly, hiding behind his mother's skirts that first week as if we were strangers. He seemed to be warning us: do not take my trust for granted. For most of that year, Tom was madly, deeply in love with both baseball and Disney's *Snow White*. To please him, I purchased a copy of the book with pictures from the movie for the classroom. For weeks it was his constant companion. I'd find it carefully placed beside him in the block corner or manipulatives area. At playground time, I'd find him furtively tucking it under the papers in his cubby to prevent other children from choosing it from the bookshelves later at rest time. I can still remember him on his cot at rest time, studying the book, wearing his Chicago Cubs cap, tracing the pictures with his fingers.

While Tom's intensity charmed me more every day, I knew that the "Should we retain him?" question would inevitably arise, since Tom was barely five (Chicago's cut-off date is in December). His late birthday and his below average reading and writing sub-skills were the prevailing criteria for retention in kindergarten then, as they are now. What can you say about a five-year-old boy whose intelligence and verve were apparent in the block corner, at the game table, and on our makeshift baseball diamond, but who hated all activities that involved pencil and paper? That he "wasn't ready to learn" or that my classroom wasn't ready for him?

That winter I read Sylvia Ashton-Warner's *Teacher*. Her inspiring approach included asking the children to tell her a word that they wished to write that day. These words became the kids' personal vocabulary bank. One week I allowed myself to take a break from the skill-based worksheets to try her idea. On Monday I wrote what the children told me on sturdy strips of card stock. Then the children copied the words. Tom first asked to write *baseball* and then *baseball game*. On Thursday or Friday, as I approached his table, Tom began to laugh and called out, "Strawberry." (At the time, I didn't know why it tickled him so, but it did. I assume now he was referring to the baseball player Darryl Strawberry. Not being as knowledgeable in this field as five-year-old boys, I missed the joke.) In any case, Ashton-Warner's idea was working: Tom was writing without protest, even caring about the shape of his letters.

The next week, on a hunch, I copied the first page of the Snow White book Tom loved so much. It filled a sheet of lined paper. I showed Tom what I had done and told him that for writing that day he could copy as much from my sheet as he wished. It took him a week of Table Time, but he wrote every last word, even though he could barely read a single one. Tom was happy and proud. I was intrigued by his breakthrough. Baseball and Snow White made it possible for Tom to tolerate writing, at least in the physical sense. It was the beginning of my understanding that I could rely on what children already knew and cared about to teach them something new, to overcome obstacles such as a resistance to writing.

But, lest the reader think I was now a teacher transformed, the truth is that vocabulary banks and copying from one's favorite books were the exception rather than the norm during my first year as a kindergarten teacher. I doubt that I provided Tom with enough opportunities to explore what he really had to say during his kindergarten year. At the time, I wasn't sure what the measurable academic value of these more personal writing activities were. I had never heard of a "writer's voice," and my lack of experience meant that I could only accept on faith Ashton-Warner's belief in the connection between a child's own language and his or her reading and writing development. In any case, these small successes didn't satisfy my sense of obligation to prepare Tom and his classmates for first grade. Shouldn't something more concrete be required for this formidable task? The one thing I was certain of, however, was that both Tom and I enjoyed our special activities far more than we enjoyed printing the letters of the alphabet in neat rows.

❦ *Weighing Our Options*

By my second year in the classroom, I began to worry that my lack of appreciation for the traditional and formal lessons of kindergarten would eventually drive me out of the profession. How could I hate most what I felt most responsible to teach? In retrospect, I see that while I weighed my options, I didn't realize that there, at the start of their school lives, the kids were weighing their own: many of them had already opted out, deciding to separate completely their real lives from their school lives.

Over the course of my first few years as a teacher, of watching the Toms, Merediths, and De Juans come and go, I felt the stirrings of change. For one thing, it became clear that many, if not most, of my children did not learn to read through a strictly phonics/letter reproduction approach. Each year brought children who were already reading, though they had never had the benefit of formal phonetic instruction. Other children had mastered phonics, but were not readers. I sent them off to first grade for more of the same. I had not identified any child as a "writer." With experience, I was also becoming more vocal about my concerns as a teacher.

Were learning to read and write *necessarily* boring or repressive experiences? Why didn't beginning reading and writing education satisfy like the block corner or the housekeeping center?

Or stories? As a young teacher, I was delighted, though I must admit surprised, at the level of interest stories held for children from all backgrounds. Unlike the academic activities at table time, story time seemed to make everyone successful (not too different from their reaction to my co-teacher's singing and guitar playing, another non-academic area of learning that in recent years has received due recognition for its contribution to the reading and writing process.) Stories clearly had some potential beyond their relationship to language development. This potential could be cultivated for its part in the reading and writing process. Tom's interest in writing down the first page of *Snow White* had demonstrated that. However, I had yet to discover anything systematic about the uses of stories and reading and writing.

It seemed that even in the best pre-school classrooms real books and stories were limited to morning story time. First and second grade teachers told me that the ritual had all but disappeared from the daily curriculum. Almost no teachers talked about telling stories or having children write their own stories. As for my own classroom, the morning picture book reading was a great pleasure, but not indispensable, competing as it often did with the fireman's visit, or a special art activity, or a too long table time. I had yet to protect stories from interruptions in the curriculum in the same way that I scheduled special activities around the morning table time and so-called academic work. Since it was increasingly clear, however, that the children did not view our phonics-based reading and writing activities as reading and writing in any real sense, I began to wonder what the point was in sticking with it so tenaciously. Furthermore, I had begun to realize that one book a day could not infuse a child with a sense of story, or create an interest in other people's stories, as described by Robert Coles in his book *The Call of Stories*. I longed for this to happen because this alone could provide the motivation to become a reader and writer at any cost—even of worksheets!

About this same time, it was oral storytelling, not reading aloud, that got me interested in the relationship between stories and reading and writing. In my first few years of teaching, I found that children rarely asked me to tell them a story. Read one, yes. Listening to original stories simply wasn't part of their experience, at least not their school experience. (By kindergarten many of these children had been in school for three or four years.)

Making up stories for young children, however, was an old trick of mine from my babysitting days, which I often had used as a time filler until their parents returned home. The stories themselves weren't very good. Although I managed to maintain a basic plot structure (undoubtedly the benefit of all my years of reading and listening to stories), for the most part they were short and trite, and worked off a one-joke punch line. Characterization of any kind was absent, but this didn't seem to matter to the children, especially when I created characters named after them. Invariably, the children would then demand stories with "their names in it."

I started making up stories for my kindergartners both to fill the need for a transition between indoor and outdoor periods and simply to make the kids laugh after a long morning of teacher dos and don'ts—nothing more. In fact, storytelling seemed so playful to me that when I introduced it into our kindergarten classroom I didn't even think to include it in my formal curriculum plans.

If my educational intentions in telling children's stories were unclear, the children's responses were anything but. The children's enthusiasm for my silly stories was indisputable. By my third year of teaching, I could see a familiar pattern in their reactions. At first, they were curious. Once they were drawn in, they became intensely focused during the story. I couldn't help but notice the deep interest, better than joy, in their faces, and they begged for more. They especially liked stories with jokes about themselves, and with issues that weren't too close to home. For example, they would not have enjoyed a vivid description of an angry mother, but they adored the story in which the janitor had mistakenly replaced their table chairs with those from the toddler room. They howled as I depicted them, in great confusion, trying to reach the high table from so far down.

Over time I realized that the absence of a book, toy, or lesson during storytelling allowed me to share myself with the children much more honestly and directly. Despite the playful mood, I felt somewhat vulnerable during storytelling, as if I were taking a risk. The risk was more than simple accountability, however; it was emotional. There we were, eye to eye, naked almost. But the circle of children—some dark, some light, some well-dressed, some in need of a bath, all so alive—returned the favor of my risk by falling in love with me, my silly stories, and story time. Quite unlike our phonics lessons, these storytelling sessions felt scary and thrilling, but they made me glad to be a teacher.

💥 *Stories for Children Who Have Failed*

In 1983, due to family circumstances, I took a job as a long-term substitute teacher for a class in a relatively poor school on eastern Long Island whose teacher had taken an emergency medical leave. The principal told me little except that I would have a class of eighteen children who were chronologically eligible for third grade, but who were all reading well below grade level. I remember that he very carefully pointed out that none of the children had tested learning-disabled in any way. "Why can't they read?" I asked. He shrugged his shoulders.

I soon learned the principal was right. The children couldn't read anywhere near grade level. My job, according to the school district reading specialists, was to instruct them in the DISTAR method (Direct Instruction Teaching Arithmetic and Reading). In actuality, DISTAR was only the first of four programs in a six-month period that I was told to use with the children. There was no mention of dropping one program for the other. "Give up science," a co-teacher suggested when I complained of a lack of time. No one seemed to wonder about the absurdity of four different phonics-based programs to serve one problem. Again, there was no mention of writing of any kind. All four programs were far more mind numbing than any phonics worksheet I had seen in kindergarten. All used controlled vocabularies and contrived stories, though DISTAR was by far the worst. DISTAR even came with a prepared set of questions for the teacher. I'll never forget my disbelief when I perused the Teacher's Guide. There in blue ink were the words I was to say. The children's responses were printed in black (or vice versa). How could the authors dare to predict what children would say? I wondered, still somewhat naïve in the world of educational quick-fixes. The teacher's script had been written in such a way that it elicited the exact, stated response from the children. The first time it happened I stared at the children in disbelief. If it didn't feel a little like a scene from Orwell's *1984*, it could have been funny.

It didn't surprise me that the children made little progress in the first couple of months. Who could, any reasonable person might argue, when the morning's story included sentences such as "The tramp tamped the ramp with his lamp." What did this mean? The Teacher's Guide said something about "phonetic families."

One day I brought in a Liza Minnelli album because of a song I wanted to try out on the kids. I wrote her name on the board and pronounced it several times, pointing to the syllables with a ruler. Many kids in the class were Italian or hispanic and the last name gave them no trouble. There was a dark-haired little girl named Liza in the class, however. We talked about the name Liza, about how it was slightly different than the more popular Lisa, but easy to mistake for it if you read too quickly. Apparently, there were several Lisas in the other classes, and our Liza was continually being mixed up with them. I then played the song "Liza with a Z," an hilarious account of Minnelli's frustration with having her name mispronounced all of her life. How could the children help but get the point, with such detailed lyrics as "It's Liza with a *z*, not Lisa with an *s*, 'cause Liza with a *z* goes *zzz* not *sss*"? And "If I were *Ruth* then I'd be *Ruth*, because with *Ruth* what can you do? Or Kathy or Susan. . . ." The song goes on, and just when Minnelli seems to convince the listener she just can't take it anymore, she hears someone say, "Look, there she goes— Liza—Min*nulli*." A very funny lesson in double consonants follows next.

The children responded with shrieks of laughter. I had to play the song two more times. It was clear that at least some of them were beginning to understand that reading was, in part, determined by the sounds of the letters, and, in part, by assumptions about what the words on the page might say. *Liza* could easily be misread as *Lisa*, and vice versa, depending on whether you read the consonant correctly or let your expectations guide you. This was an important lesson for a group of kids who had been taught that real reading always followed strict rules, an understandable position, given their usual reading fare. I was congratulating myself on being such a clever teacher, when Derrick asked, "How did they (meaning the record company, presumably) know about Liza?" I realized immediately that he meant Liza R., the eight-year-old in our class, not Liza Minnelli. The song was so relevant, so pertinent to his experience, that he thought it had been written for our class. He had created a story to fit what he knew.

From the beginning I told the children stories, despite the overloaded schedule, and they loved them as much as my kindergarten children had in Chicago. The themes of these stories were not the same, of course. Five-year-olds are interested in appearing much older than three- and four-year-olds, or in the time of castles, kings, and queens, or in the silly consequences of putting your clothes on backwards. Eight- and nine-year-olds prefer stories about realistic mysteries and challenges. I set these stories on the wharves and fishing boats that dotted the eastern shore of Long Island, where many of these children's parents were employed. Another difference in making up stories for eight-, nine-, and ten-year-olds was that they became very intrigued with the process of storytelling itself. How did I know those things, they demanded? How could I make them up? I talked about how I find story materials in things that people care about, or that happen every day, and then I add a twist of mystery or silliness or sadness. They listened to my explanations as if these, too, were stories.

Eventually the kids, or at least most of them, began to make some progress in reading and writing, as evidenced not by the workbook tests, but by their abilities to read a passage from a book to me. The "Liza with a Z" lesson became a model for most phonetic problems, while the kids became storytellers themselves. However, many of them had the poor handwriting skills that are characteristic of "low achievers," and they preferred oral storytelling to writing. I let them do both.

My experience with this very special group of children was capped when, towards the end of the year, I was evaluated by the principal. He arrived during the science period, which was rotten luck for me, or so I thought until Erin answered my question about salmon swimming upstream to die. Actually, she didn't answer it, she expanded on it, by telling us how her grandmother was dying and had come home from a nursing home. She was sort of like the salmon, Erin said, because even though it would have been easier for her in the nursing home, she just wanted to be home near all of her children and grandchildren. I listened, taking pleasure in this quiet little girl's intuitive grasp of human nature. I must say I also took some credit for her burgeoning narrative skills. Surely the principal would be impressed. I received the school district's equivalent of excellent on my evaluation with the comment: "Should work on helping children stick to the topic."

🌿 *Whole Language*

In the mid-eighties the Whole Language movement, with its integrated approach to the teaching of reading and writing, started gaining momentum. Its tremendous popularity on the conference and lecture circuit, as well as with educational publishers, bears witness to this.

Whole Language deserves attention in any discussion of stories in the classroom for, without a doubt, it is the first movement in reading and writing education that has effectively included stories from children's literature in the curriculum. Let me also add that what follows is but a brief analysis of a complicated subject—indeed, far more complicated than many administrators and teachers realize, which is why the implementation of a Whole Language curriculum sometimes does not go very smoothly or produce the desired results. My intention is not to analyze the entire Whole Language movement, but merely to set classroom storytelling in the context of this powerful trend in education.

Whole Language advocates such as Ken Goodman, Yetta Goodman, Michael Sampson, Elizabeth Sulzby, William H. Teale, Shirley Raines, and Robert Canaday feel that learning to read and write is nothing less than a matter of the psycholinguistic and sociolinguistic influences on children's awareness of print. While this is often summarized as a Whole Language "philosophy," the term itself is probably too general for all theorists. Classroom teachers, however, rarely have time to worry about fine distinctions; Whole Language and its counterpart, the writing process, are the buzzwords in the faculty lounge.

Teachers who received their training prior to the rise of Whole Language will often ask, "But what does it *look* like?" In practice, Whole Language is hard to define in typical curriculum terms because in its purest sense it is more of an attitude than a prescription. According to Raines and Canaday in *The Whole Language Kindergarten*, a Whole Language classroom is one "where there is an emphasis on listening, speaking, reading, and writing . . . and meaningful communication."[2]

While true Whole Language proponents give no easy answer to the "What do I do on Monday morning?" question, they do urge teachers to foster reading and writing where real learning occurs for young children: in activities that reflect what the children are interested in. I remember Meredith from my first kindergarten class, sitting at the table, frozen in her attempts to finish her worksheet, looking silently over at the housekeeping corner where "real life" was occurring. What might I have done to bring her reading lesson into that housekeeping corner, helping her discover the best of both worlds? I once heard a pre-kindergarten teacher observe a child's reaction to finding a copy of Maurice Sendak's *Where the Wild Things Are*, which the teacher had read aloud earlier that day, and a small wooden boat, both in the housekeeping area. It seems he immediately began to act like Max, the little boy in the story who acted like a wild thing and was banished to his room, only to sail away to an imaginary land of wild things. His teacher noted that the boy's opportunity to stand up boldly and exclaim *"Be still!"* to those wild things (his friends in the nearby block corner) symbolized several important goals in her Whole Language classroom. First, it stimulated his desire to test, like Max, societal limits and rules. Second, in his imitation of Max the little boy learned something about *the application of literature to real life*. Third, after the children had a chance to explore the meaning of the text, she found *Where the Wild Things Are* to be rich in academic lessons for four-year-olds: later on the class discussed the rhyming sounds ("'Oh, please don't go. We love you so.' But Max said, 'No!'"). Then the teacher pointed out the letters that make up that wonderful event called a "rumpus." ("Let the wild rumpus start!"[3]) Academics never felt so good, she said.

By contrast, an example of an activity antithetical to the Whole Language movement would be finding objects that start with one of the letter sounds. In 1992, I observed this activity in a first grade, a kindergarten, a pre-kindergarten, and a nursery school room—all in separate schools. I heard later that the nursery school teacher eventually abandoned the task; apparently, the three-year-olds wouldn't pay attention. The fact is that while naming objects that start with the sound of a particular letter may tell three- to six-year-olds something about that sound, it can hardly tell them about themselves, or the world they live in and will one day inherit. The real contribution of the Whole Language approach to reading and writing education is that it reverses the traditional curriculum of form over function. It works from the premise that children will eventually master reading and writing, *if their minds and hearts become engaged with the real-world possibilities of reading and writing*. This is the lesson that the young Max imitator provides. When literature is that meaningful, objects that start with the letter *n* or *k* or *f* or *b* will no longer be relevant information in the reading and writing curriculum.

For all of these reasons, Whole Language is exactly what the doctor ordered: a healthy antidote of real stories, real language, and real writing to combat the unengaging world of a phonics-based curriculum. Best of all is its use of books and stories at the heart of the reading and writing curriculum. It was in this same quest for meaning in the reading and writing curriculum that I myself began using Vivian Paley's dictation and dramatization activities in my classroom, which I describe in chapter four, "When Young Children Dictate and Dramatize Their Own Stories."

❦ Cracks in the Wall

It is important to keep in mind how strongly classroom teachers are influenced by the issue of accountability, especially in reading and writing. This fear allows certain educational trends to run our professional lives—as it had made me accept the Back to Basics approach years ago—and allows some publishers to capitalize on how-to methods of teaching reading and writing. Since these trends often dominate conferences, workshops, publishers' materials, and state-adopted curricula, teachers must be particularly savvy in locating the theory behind the materials. Likewise, the popularization of any classroom idea is bound to create some misuse, often because the idea is interpreted too rigidly.

If there is a problem with the Whole Language approach, I think it began when examples used in the theory of how children learn to read and write were mistakenly seen as prescriptions for practice, calling for specific guidelines and activities. This allowed thoughtless publishers to promote materials that promised to create Whole Language classrooms, when in fact only a teacher can create a Whole Language classroom. Real Whole Language defies mass production.

Whole Language classrooms typically emphasize reading and writing lessons that are derived from real stories rather than basal readers. Few interested in children's development as storytellers or readers and writers would argue with this. The problem with a so-called literature-based curriculum occurs when lessons *not related to the story itself* drive the children's experience of that story, under the name of some skill such as prediction or beginning sounds. For example, in the Macmillan Whole Language Big Books series, the publishers claim that a book such as *Eeny, Meeny, Miney, Mouse* provides experience with literature while it helps build these essential reading skills: "letter recognition, building sight vocabulary, recognizing colors, numbers and shapes, identification of vowels and consonants, visual and auditory discrimination, time concepts and spatial relationships, sequencing skills, phonics abilities, comprehension, sorting and classifying." These reading skills, however, are not the result of merely reading the story, but of the pre- and post-story lessons that the publisher provides, which closely resemble a basics approach. *Eeny, Meeny, Miney, Mouse* is a simple picture book with a slight text. "Eeny, meeny, miney, munch. Have you been nibbling cheese for lunch?" is followed by "Eeny, meeny, miney, mums. Have you been spreading cookie crumbs?" and so on. It is appealing, but it does not stand up to the prescribed week's worth of lessons, which range from "getting in a mouse mood" to searching for all the words that end in *i-n-g*. Ironically, in many ways these interpretations of Whole Language theory have come to resemble exactly what a Whole Language approach attempts to avoid.

Publishers aren't the only ones at fault, either. Teachers must take some responsibility for curriculum. Consider the very popular book, *Brown Bear, Brown Bear*, by Bill Martin, Jr. It has been my experience that children between one and four adore *Brown Bear, Brown Bear*. In the story, an unseen character asks the brown bear and other animals what they "see" just around the corner. The story ends with a mother "seeing" all the beautiful children, proving once again that children will not (or cannot) stray too far from mother's watchful eye. (A 1991 version has revised the ending to substitute a teacher for the mother.) *Brown Bear, Brown Bear* is sometimes touted for its teaching of colors—each animal is a different color. (Oddly enough, the color reproductions in the original edition were muddy, but the 1991 version corrected this.) The book's great appeal to the toddlers, however, is found in its underlying theme more than anything else. It truly engages them because it addresses the things they think about: in this case, separation and reunion.

Whole Language specialists value books such as *Brown Bear, Brown Bear* for their predictable language ("Brown bear, brown bear, what do you see? I see a red bird looking at me. Red bird, red bird, what do you see? I see a yellow duck looking at me."), especially "their familiar content and structure, and the often repetitious, cyclical sequencing."[4] Indeed, *Brown Bear, Brown Bear*—along with other predictable books—has become a staple in many Whole Language kindergartens. Its popularity as a base for other whole language experiences, in fact, far exceeds its place as a mere story. For example, many teachers have children make their own versions of it by substituting themselves and their friends or whatever they choose for the brown bear and the other animals. In the several different kindergartens where I have observed this activity, I have never seen it offered as *optional*. I have even seen it where children choose from a set of dittoed animals or other figures, rather than make their own illustrations. I have never seen it as an open-ended activity where the child could stray from the original format.

In my view, this is hardly "meaningful communication" in the best Whole Language tradition—it is a worksheet by any other name. The child is not at the center of this activity, the product is. To top it off, I doubt seriously that *Brown Bear, Brown Bear* is a particularly interesting book to kindergarteners. It's far better suited to younger children. Almost all kindergartners know their colors, and they are at an age when developmental concerns are not focused on separation issues, but family relationships in general, making friends, and becoming more accomplished. I don't see how kindergarten teachers can justify spending a week's worth of language arts time on it.

I should point out that generic cut-and-paste or "draw a picture of" activities are not limited to the early childhood curriculum, and existed long before the arrival of Whole Language. But given their stranglehold on the early childhood classroom, it is easy to see how publishers and teachers have allowed Whole Language to be subsumed into this simplistic view of learning. Take the ubiquitous Fall Leaves unit. How many thousands and thousands of young American children celebrate the beginning of autumn by drawing pictures of leaves or coloring dittoes of them? All pre-packaged teacher materials on weather come with a Fall Leaves display, depicting, again, red, yellow, and orange leaves. Yet while teacher materials for weather units may be similar across the nation, the weather isn't. Millions of American children never have experienced and never will experience a New England fall, do not find red and yellow and orange leaves on their nature walks, and do not observe squirrels gathering up nuts among great piles of brilliantly colored foliage. Yet this formal lesson in Fall Leaves is as common as juice time in our nation's pre-school and primary grades. It may be mildly interesting to young children that other regions of the country experience such tangible beauty, but how about their own backyards, or their own school playgrounds?

Picture books, like the weather, are personal experiences. Children should be asked to respond to what they know, see, and feel about them, but it is wrong to insist on a single rigid interpretation of them that ignores the actual children in the classroom.

Lack of Confidence in the Power of Stories

As I see it, half the problem in using literature to teach reading and writing has been a lack of confidence in the story experience itself. While educators say that children *like* to hear stories, we don't always appreciate the inherent academic value of *listening* to stories. Instead, we impose on stories a myriad of objective-driven activities that can prevent the fulfillment of the young child's role as listener and beneficiary of stories and the many academic lessons to be gained indirectly.

In far too many classrooms, in the name of Whole Language, listening to stories is accompanied by a set of formal questions asking the children to predict from the pictures what will happen next or to change the ending. A case study in *The Whole Language Kindergarten* describes one such situation:

> When Kathy [a Whole Language teacher in training] recalled the read-aloud activities she had seen when she visited the Whole Language classrooms, she remembered that many of the teachers brainstormed with the children and discussed several ideas related to the book, before beginning to read the story. One teacher spent almost five minutes having the children tell what they already knew about the two characters, Frog and Toad, before she read to

them. Then the children looked at (sampled) the picture and print on the outside cover of the book to make predictions about the story. As the teacher read to the children she paused periodically to let the children confirm that their predictions were accurate or to change their predictions, as they heard new information in the story.[5]

Studies have shown that the way parents and children interact when reading stories together plays a significant role in a child's early literacy development. My guess is that, in the scenario above, the teacher was trying to replicate that interaction. Few parents I know, however, ask their child to predict what will happen next in the story, or check to see how well their child understood the story, except in the most general terms ("Did you like that story?" and not "Why do you think Big Anthony wanted to use Strega Nona's magic pot?").

When I watch self-described Whole Language teachers select a new story, and then proceed to ask the class six or seven questions about the story (which the children haven't even heard yet), ask them to make predictions based on the title or the pictures, or stop the story to ask the children what will happen next or why they think a certain character is behaving in a certain way, I want to shout: "Down in front! You're blocking our view!" If stories are naturally appealing to the young children, then why not let them have a natural life? With each rereading, and some carefully placed explanations by the teacher, the children will understand a little better. Teachers should also give the children the chance to invent their own questions ("Does anyone have any questions about what happened to Big Anthony?").

Of course, not all stories are worth repeating. Teachers need to watch for stories that "catch on," stories that fulfill some deep understanding of human intentions, or express a developmental concern, or arouse our curiosity: these are the stories that should lead a curriculum of hearing stories, knowing them, and—if they appeal—reliving them through writing, drama, or retelling. These are the stories that would bear up under a select few academic lessons. These are the activities that should constitute a true literature-based curriculum.

❧ *Whole Language, Dictation, and Writing*

In recent years, our understanding of how young children become writers has taken some enormous leaps. The traditional "learning to print" approach has given way to one that stresses learning to write as real writers are said to do. We now see classrooms in which children regularly write journals, notes, messages, poems, and stories. These are exciting classrooms to be in. Whole Language, together with the writing process movement (in its less prescriptive forms), has contributed much to this progress in the writing curriculum.

At the same time, in some classrooms, I see a growing insistence on certain approaches to writing that seem inappropriate to many children under eight. It should not be assumed that what children are capable of at ten and twelve years old, they are also capable of at eight or six or four. If a phonics-based, scope-and-sequence curriculum puts reading and writing into neat little patterns that defy what we know about reading and writing, some popular writing techniques defy what we know about child development. Take story writing. Before we ask young children to write their stories, they must first learn about writing stories as something real people do. The Russian psychologist Lev S. Vygotsky wrote that development, or mastery, is preceded by learning, and learning will always involve some degree of imitation of more competent others.[6] In other words, in order to become writers young children must have plenty of opportunity to observe and imitate people writing, including teachers, older children, and, ideally, parents. In some classrooms, however, children's understanding of where stories come from is taken for granted. Instead of modeling for children, teachers begin with simply finding the right topic. Since many five-, six-, seven-, and eight-year-olds without prior experience in story writing don't really understand the relationship between what they can imagine and what can be written down, many "pre-writing" or "brainstorming" sessions don't prepare them for the next step: writing. The fact is that beginning writers don't write because they have something they want to say, they write in order to discover what they have to say, just as they play with blocks, and on the playground, letting the ideas just flow. This is why I see dictation as so valuable to the young storyteller. Subtly and over time, dictation helps teach the child-author that a written story is merely an oral one put into print. Dictation also helps demystify the orthographic features of print, such as the movement of words from left to right, top to bottom, the space between words, punctuation marks, and so on, because it offers the child an opportunity to scrutinize the way in which words come out of the teacher's pen. The child's investment in his or her own story is what keeps him or her interested in the page of writing. (I discuss in more detail the value of dictation in chapter four, "When Young Children Dictate and Dramatize Their Own Stories.")

Just as the goal of having children write independently may ignore their lack of experience in writing, the goal of having children under eight or nine revise their work also may ignore some fundamental issues about children this young. True revision relies on some understanding that you can change a piece for the better. It requires a sense of letting go for the sake of improvement. From a developmental perspective, most children under eight, however, don't like change, and may view the teacher's desire for revision as criticism. In cases where they are to rewrite the piece on their own, revision only adds to what was already a physically demanding chore for children this young. Finally, for many children under eight, yesterday's work is old news. They are simply not interested in working on it further.

Invented Spelling

Another technique meant to empower young writers that runs the risk of backfiring—especially when overemphasized—is invented spelling. Of all the ideas that have emanated from the current research in reading and writing, including Whole Language, invented spelling is probably the most prevalent in pre-school and primary grade classrooms.

In my opinion, there is a place for invented spelling in any progressive writing curriculum. Children younger than eight hardly can be expected to know how to spell every word they can say. They should have every opportunity to guess at how words are spelled, throughout the curriculum. When they're writing, they should be aware that spelling can be corrected later. The most important thing young writers should learn is that the idea counts above all. The problem with invented spelling comes when teachers insist on its use at all times. I have observed this attitude more often than I care to admit. For example, in response to a pre-kindergarten child asking, "Teacher, how do you spell *hospital*?" her teacher answered, "Spell it the way it sounds." When the child looked a little dismayed, the teacher next asked, "How do *you* think it should be spelled?" It was clear that the child did not have the answer to her own question, so how could she answer the teacher's? These should not be rote responses, given in the name of making children feel good about their own immaturity. Given automatically, without reflection on the child before us, these responses don't acknowledge the possibility that the child *needs* to know the correct answer for reasons beyond his or her writing development. I find that when a child does not accept, or appears frustrated with, an insistence of invented spelling, there is often a tie-in to his or her understanding of rules in general, as well as a growing awareness that words have a correct and incorrect spelling.

Briefly, we know that young children grow into an appreciation of rules as standards for behavior. In the process, they go from appearing oblivious to rules to insisting on rules for rules' sake, somewhere between four and seven. Later, when children develop a fuller understanding of the rule's purpose, they relax their control. The development of young children's relationship to rules is a fascinating process, and it affects their learning in all areas, from language development to science to board games. The same young children who played games such as Candy Land or Chutes and Ladders with their own idiosyncratic sense of what was required eventually enjoy playing correctly—and are very attracted to games with more complicated rules such as Checkers and Monopoly. They become frustrated when younger brothers and sisters, or less mature classmates, "won't play right." On the playground or baseball field, they are busily cultivating an appreciation for not stepping on the lines, or three strikes and you're out. By six and seven and eight years old, children know that you can reach perfection in school—100—and that anything less means that something is wrong.

The same idea applies to a child's developing awareness of the rules of spelling. One first grade boy in a Whole Language classroom in Houston, for example, brought home a piece of paper on which he had completed the sentence "I like to. . . ." His read, "I like to play ball." His mother was curious. "Tony, you hate to play ball." "I know," answered Tony, "but I didn't know how to spell watch television." This interested Tony's mother, for only the year before he had had no trouble inventing the spelling of a word. In a year's time, however, he had come to the realization that words have a conventional spelling, a right way. Moreover, by first grade he knew that a word's spelling was directly tied to its readability: until he could approximate his intention more accurately, he didn't want to take the risk of being misunderstood.

Halfway across the country, in a New York public school, a new first grade teacher told me that many of her children could not carry out this same activity, which had been prescribed by her school's Whole Language specialist. They could not finish "in their own words" sentences that she gave them, such as "When it snows I like to. . . ." The children said they didn't know how to spell some of the words they wanted to include in their sentences. When she reminded them that "spelling didn't count," and pressed them to write the words "the way they sounded," they still refused. Flat out refused. The teacher, who had not been trained in Whole Language, was very frustrated. She wanted to help the children spell the words, but felt that it would undermine the "in their own words" dictum. "I thought Whole Language was not supposed to emphasize rules," she observed. "But, believe me, some of the ideas sure feel like rules. And we are not supposed to challenge them."

I felt sorry for this new teacher, and for the reading specialists in her school. I'm sure they all wanted to do right by the children. But if they were all to watch these first graders on the playground, if they could listen to them in their play, if they could hear them discuss what constitutes 100 on a test, they would know why insistence on invented spelling can stymie a beginning writer who has moved into an awareness of rules.

So when we insist spelling doesn't matter in the interest of promoting creative writing, we are often ignoring an individual child's developing sense of correctness, inadvertently creating a resistance to writing in the process. How to strike the necessary balance? Let's go back to the classroom of the first grade teacher. Regardless of where the children or the teacher stand on invented spelling, the teacher obviously can't spell every word for every child—this would set a bad precedent for future writing activities. The teacher could acknowledge the children's needs, however, by saying: "Okay, some of the words you want to write, you won't know how to spell. If you want to, guess—spell them the way you think they should be spelled. But if you want my help, let me know, and I will spell up to two words [or three or four, depending on the size of the class] for each of you. If you have more words that you're unsure of, write them down the best way you can, and underline them. As I come around I'll tell you how to spell them correctly." A response in this vein acknowledges the children's great concern about spelling, which in this case has grown to include the whole class, while it deals with the impracticality of the teacher having to spell every single word. Out of necessity, then, not unawareness, the children are encouraged to spell some words on their own.

🌿 Remaining Flexible

This is not to say that techniques such as invented spelling don't work some of the time for some children. It's just that they can't be strictly interpreted at the expense of our knowledge that a child's personal history, his or her general development, and the learning curve are all intertwined. Unless we acknowledge the relationship between learning and development, stories and the children's interest in writing their own stories will be lost in the curriculum. Their voices will be silenced.

Teachers—especially the kindergarten, first and second grade teachers—need to remain flexible in their methods in teaching reading and writing. They need to trust their own instincts and be responsive to individual students. We have waited a long time for stories and writing to be valued in the school curriculum. Let's not give them away to formulas.

My greatest worry over current practice, however, is that pre-school and primary teachers who are sincerely experimenting with new ideas, such as portfolio evaluation, may run out of time to get it right, for there are once again black clouds on the horizon. Most teachers agree that a natural or holistic approach to the teaching of reading and writing doesn't pay in test scores before third grade. Parents and administrators or state boards don't like to wait until third grade for good testing results. Nine years old, it seems, is too late to wait for cultivated, mature readers and writers. Teachers are, once again, faced with a "just in case" crisis in choosing curriculum. In some school districts, phonics instruction is regaining ground. And in some cases teachers have absolutely no other choice.

My frustration with the current state of affairs in teaching reading to young children is the reliance on activities *about* stories, rather than on stories themselves. In teaching writing to young children, I worry that we are teaching the *craft* of writing, without having helped these newcomers discover the *soul* of it. I would like to see all teachers considering the possibility that young children can become readers and writers for the sake of stories—including their own—that reflect their personal histories and their developmental stages. After all, in much the same way they learned to walk, talk, ride a bike, and play ball. The truth is that young children continually reveal to us what they know, or are in the process of knowing, about reading and writing, if only we will take the time to discover it.

---

1. Paley, Vivian, *Wally's Stories*, p. 66.
2. Raines and Canady, *The Whole Language Kindergarten*, p. 13.
3. Sendak, Maurice. *Where the Wild Things Are*.
4. Goodman, Ken, *What's Whole in Whole Language*, p. 47.
5. Raines and Canady, *The Whole Language Kindergarten*, p. 24.
6. Vygotsky, Lev S., *Mind in Society*, pp. 86–88.

Chapter Four

✼

WHEN YOUNG CHILDREN DICTATE AND DRAMATIZE THEIR OWN STORIES

The first time I asked Wally if he wanted to write a story he looked surprised.
"You didn't teach me to write yet," he said.
"You just tell me the story, Wally. I'll write the words."
. . . We acted out the story immediately . . . and a flurry of story writing be-
gan that continued and grew all year.

—Vivian Paley, *Wally's Stories*

As an experienced teacher, I know that learning the letters and sounds
of the alphabet may enable a child to decode this sentence, but probably
doesn't help that child "read" it, in the advanced sense of understanding
it. True understanding of the written word is the result of a search for
meaning. In my experience, dictating stories provides children with the
ultimate reason to seek meaning in the written word: to discover one's
own story. At first, the discovery may be accidental: "Teacher, look,
[pointing] that says my name. And there's Joey's name." Children past the
age of four or five who dictate stories on a regular basis, however, carefully observe the teacher's writing, like small detectives in search of some
great treasure: their story in words. At the same time, dictating stories
provides young storytellers with many opportunities to learn sub-skills of
reading, such as the formation of letters in a consistent manner, the pro-
gression of words from left to right and top to bottom, discrete word
spaces, and all of the other information necessary for successful decoding.

Similarly, learning to print letters is not the same as "writing" in the sense of conveying an idea. To be a writer is to control the form and function of print to communicate with the reader. Writing is an even more complex task than reading because writers not only have to be able to read print, they have to reproduce it from memory in order to say what they have to say, which can be an arduous physical and mental task for children under eight. Becoming a writer, like becoming a reader, relies mostly on an experienced adult's inviting a child into the process. In my experience, becoming a storyteller—in the sense of using a recognizable format—is the first step in becoming a writer. An invitation to dictate a story is a great way to begin this process for the child.

My understanding of young children's early literacy development improved enormously the year I started using Vivian Paley's dictation activities in my kindergarten classroom. Following Paley's lead, I also used the complementary activity, dramatization of both adult-authored and child-authored stories. I've come to appreciate their value to young children's development as readers and writers, as I used them in my own classroom and as I have helped other teachers use them in theirs. In my work with teachers, however, I am careful to point out that my interpretation of Paley's ideas is largely that, my interpretation, based on many years' experience. In this chapter I use a simple outline of three components—dramatization of adult-authored stories, dictation, and dramatization of children's stories—to set the stage for a broader discussion of their place in the classroom. Chapter six, "A Guide to Storytelling in the Classroom," describes the process in more detail.

✿ *Dramatization of Adult-Authored Stories*

The dramatization of adult-authored stories is a well-known activity in early childhood education, but it is used in surprisingly few pre-school classrooms and in hardly any primary ones. While it lays important groundwork for the children's dictation and dramatization of their own stories, it's well worth considering as an activity with its own rightful contribution to early literacy development and the overall life of the classroom.

The first step in dramatizing adult-authored stories is for the teacher or children to choose a story to "act out." Then the teacher reads the story aloud, at least once, usually at a Group Time. When the story is finished, the teacher assigns children to play the different parts. Most teachers prefer to have the children sitting in a circle. The interior of the circle thus becomes the "stage." If the story has a large number of characters, it is better to limit the cast to a manageable size. (Besides, it is important to leave some children for the audience .) Next, the teacher rereads the story while the performers take up their roles. Their job is to interpret the text as best they can, with some help from the teacher and the audience ("How would the bad wolf sound if he were pretending to be Little Red Riding Hood's grandmother?"). In this type of dramatization, there are no rehearsals. There are rarely props. The idea is not so much one of performance, but of play. Like all good play, the drama should be spontaneous and imaginative.

Stories that please the children can be dramatized over and over again. I once directed the dramatization of *Snow White and the Seven Dwarfs* at least twelve times in a single week, changing the cast each time in order to give everyone a chance at the different parts. Paley said that her kindergarten class dramatized *The Tinder Box* seventeen times over the course of the year. When faced with time constraints, one kindergarten teacher I know has three casts acting simultaneously in different corners of the room. The important thing is to satisfy the children's desire to experiment with trading roles. Of course, some stories don't appeal to the children as much as others, and they don't ask for them to be repeated.

When selecting stories to dramatize, teachers should keep in mind that some stories lend themselves better to this type of dramatization than others, especially in the beginning. *The Carrot Seed,* for example, works wonderfully for all ages on a first try, whereas I found *The Ugly Duckling* far too cumbersome. Also, a story with too much dialogue will not be successful without some modification of parts. Young children can hardly be expected to memorize their lines. The same goes for lengthy narrative descriptions, which the teacher may want to shorten in order to keep the action flowing.

The dramatization of adult-authored stories accomplishes three goals. First, it provides the children with a model of "book language" and story form. Second, it furthers the presence of stories in the classroom: once young children have had the regular experience of dramatizing stories, they will invariably think to dramatize a new one, thus becoming players as well as listeners in the world of stories. Finally, it sets the tone for dramatization of the children's own stories.

❦ *Children Dictating Their Own Stories*

Dictation allows each child the opportunity to tell his or her story to the teacher. The stories can be original or borrowed (from friends, the media, or a book). The teacher should feel free to ask whatever questions are necessary to help the child express himself or herself ("Matthew, do you mean to say the kids went to sleep in Alaska?" "No, no. They got on a plane and went home and *then* they went to sleep."). The teacher's role in taking dictation is a complicated one. Primarily, she must strive to understand what the child intends to say in his or her story, and write it down accordingly. To do so, she must balance the scales carefully between scribe and facilitator.

In practical terms, my experience has been that children generally take from three to twelve minutes to dictate their stories, depending, of course, on the age and interest of the child. I encourage teachers to ask children to tell their stories in a regular rotation, which gives everyone the same chance. Dictation should also occur on a regular basis, at least two or three times a week. Some teachers take stories every day. A reasonable goal is to give the youngest children at least one turn every two weeks and the older ones a turn every three or four weeks. Classrooms with twenty to twenty-five children simply can't squeeze any more time out of the schedule. While the wait may be a little long between stories for the other kids, they learn a great deal from observing and listening to their classmates tell stories, as well as in the subsequent opportunity to dramatize their classmates' stories. Most teachers find it practical to impose a one-page limit on the stories. This is a sensitive point with teachers and writers who fear that the artificial limit will inhibit the children's creativity. I've never observed this to be a problem. Younger children seem to run out of steam after ten or more minutes of storytelling (some are done in less than two minutes). Older children, who often have much more to say than a page allows, are routinely offered the opportunity to close with "to be continued," a convention they are familiar with from television and chapter books. The one-page limit helps the teacher budget her time for other children to have a chance. After twenty or more minutes at the storytelling table, some teachers understandably begin to get anxious about returning to the group at large. Activities that don't account for other classroom realities will not be popular with teachers. A one-page limit may be a little artificial, but the tradeoff is a classroom where all the children have the opportunity to tell stories.

❦ *Dramatization of the Children's Stories*

Child-authored dramatization follows the same format as that of the adult-authored dramatization except that most teachers I work with prefer that the author, not the teacher, choose the classmates who will be in his or her cast. Paley has revised her views on this subject. Now, in the interest of fairness, the roles in her students' stories are distributed on the basis of who's next on the list. Paley describes the events that led up to this decision in her book, *You Can't Say You Can't Play.* Fairness, of course, is a central interest of young children, and Paley's book has great implications for early childhood education. But many teachers I have talked to about the matter of fairness in the assignment of roles in the dramatization process by and large still vote in favor of the author making the final decision. They seem to feel that choosing one's own cast represents the only area in which children have any real control in the classroom. I urge teachers to watch the selection process carefully. If some children are being excluded routinely, then some intervention such as Paley's list may be needed, at least until the pattern is broken.

The dramatization of child-authored stories is not usually repeated, for the simple reason they don't need to be. Experiencing them once with the class seems to be enough. There is no reason, however, that the teacher and children couldn't repeat these dramatizations.

As in adult-authored dramatization, if the text includes dialogue, the actors repeat it after the teacher. The teacher might offer technical assistance ("Show us what you look like when you eat breakfast"). The children in the audience might offer helpful suggestions ("*Close your eyes when you're sleeping*"). Faithfulness to the text, and not a polished, uninterrupted performance, is the priority.

❦ *Informal Learning in Dictation and Dramatization*

One day as I was writing down five-year-old Miko's story, it began to dawn on me that children could acquire some formal knowledge about reading and writing without acquiring it in a formal activity. Miko's buddy Colin was standing beside him, watching, waiting for Miko to finish so that they could resume their play in the block area. They were a delightful duo, these two, but different in many ways. Miko was small and round, Japanese, the youngest son in a family that had temporarily immigrated so that the father could earn a Ph.D. Colin was very tall, slim, black.

He was the oldest of four boys, well cared for in a single family home, but not without the attendant problems of poverty. Unsurprisingly, Miko demonstrated the behaviors we typically associate with bright children: highly verbal, inquisitive, creative, a leader. Colin had recently been classified as Educable Mentally Handicapped by the local public school that he would enter as a first grader. They loved each other dearly.

It was the fall of the first school year that I took down children's stories. This was the third story that Miko had dictated to me. (Although Colin had had the opportunity, he had declined thus far to tell a story.) As I wrote down Miko's story, I looked up and found Colin watching me write. As I continued to write, I observed Colin out of the corner of my eye, as first he watched Miko saying the words, then me writing, then my pencil, then the paper, and then Miko again. He watched as closely as if he were following the ball at a tennis match. His face was steady, his body calm, his eyes fixed on the small field of myself, my paper and pen, and his friend. Perhaps I was especially interested in Colin's reaction because of his recent special education classification. I remember wondering, "Could a child who is so curious, so obviously intrigued by writing, really be 'slow'?" It wasn't even his story, yet he was fixated by the act of writing it down. Why? Colin may not have been learning his alphabet or phonetic sounds like his kindergarten classmates had, but how could I ignore the fact that he was learning—or at least discovering—something at this moment? It suddenly occurred to me that children don't automatically know where stories come from. I've since realized that discovering the source of stories is crucial to becoming a writer. It's a lesson that children learn best from other children, as Colin learned from Miko that fall. I treasure children's dictation for this opportunity to learn.

✖ *Borrowing*

The story Miko told also made me aware of something else about Miko and early literacy development.

Miko's Story   *October 21*

Mine is about a boy whose name is Leckerd. And he was playing with my ball with me. And he was playing and playing until he lost the ball. And he find it because he saw it in a hole. Bye-bye.

Miko's choice of topic didn't surprise me. The children in our Chicago neighborhood often played in the alleys behind their apartment buildings. I suspected that Miko's story was an interpretation of some encounter with an older child there. What surprised me was the way the image of falling into a hole in Miko's story resurfaced in his own and many of the other children's stories for weeks afterwards. I cannot account for why certain images, such as that of falling in a hole, get picked up by other children in the room. I suspect, however, that the original author has stumbled onto an image that appeals to many of the children on some primordial level.

Justin's Story   October 28

It's about me and Matthew and Miko. Me and Matthew and Miko were walking. Then there was a snake. A man came. Me and Miko and Matthew fell in a hole. Miko tried to get out. Then a monster came. It was King Kong. And he helped us out of the hole. And then we went to a spooky house. Then we saw a bat. Then we went home. Then the monster was after us. Then we ate lunch. The End.

Miko's Story   October 28

Mine is about Suke, and me, and Matthew, and Andrew, and Damien. We were walking on the street to get across the river. Then we fell in a deep, deep, deep hole. Then Matthew tried to get out. Then we saw mommy and daddy. Then we had a ladder from my daddy. Then we climbed up. Then we were safe. Bye-bye. Then we went home.

Elizabeth, not to be outdone by the boys, offered her version of falling in a hole. She also borrowed Miko's "Bye-bye" ending.

Elizabeth's Story   October 28

Once me and daddy were going Trick or Treating. We fell in a hole and there was my mommy. We lived in the hole for a couple of weeks. Then we brought a ladder and we climbed up and went back home. We went apple picking. And we saw Grandma and Granddaddy. Next Halloween it was our vacation and we fell back in our vacation hole, and we stayed for a long, long weekend. The End. Bye-bye.

Not long after this, Colin told his first story. "Oh, sure," he said matter-of-factly, when I asked him if he would like to tell me a story. His first story was only one sentence: "There was a fire in my house." His second, days later, picked up on Justin's images of snakes and of falling in a hole.

Colin's Story   November 9

One time me and my family went for a walk. Then we fell in a hole. Then we saw a snake. Then the rain killed him. Then we went home and had lunch. The End.

Children also quickly borrow story conventions from each other, such as "Once upon a time" and "The End." The fact that children borrow ideas and images from other children's stories is one of the more intriguing aspects of the dictation process. Teachers who are new to dictation are often dismayed to find that the children retell the same ideas or borrow story lines from each other. Sometimes a particular theme or character can dominate the classroom stories for months. Don't worry, it is in fact a good sign when children borrow each other's ideas. For one thing, it tells us that the children are listening to each other, validating their interest in the activities. For another, children are drawn to images that reflect some truth about themselves, as in the case of Miko's friends who fell in a hole. We should be wary of an overemphasis on originality in young children's stories, as well as in their thinking in general. What is original, anyway? Are walking, talking, reading original? There may be no one else exactly like any one of them, as they are often told by well-meaning teachers, but expecting them to think what no one else has ever thought is unfair. Young children should be free to borrow one another's ideas in their stories, to try them on, like clothes in a closet, in order to find what fits and flatters their imaginations. Each child's particular style will emerge sooner or later.

❧ Superheroes and Individuality

For most teachers who take dictation from children, the hands-down, worst-case repetition of a story is the superhero story. When I began having my students dictate stories, Star Wars characters dominated the superhero pop culture as well as the children's stories. In recent years, Teenage Mutant Ninja Turtles enjoyed an unusually long wave of popularity. In between we heard from He-Man, Ghostbusters, Batman, and others. I find that most teachers don't believe superheroes are appropriate topics for school stories; some teachers simply don't allow them. I often ask teachers I work with to discuss their rationale for this prohibition with the children. Sometimes the reason is that the teacher just doesn't feel comfortable with all that violence. (I should note that actual physical contact is not permitted in the dramatization of these stories, for the obvious safety reasons. Children have no problem observing the "No Touching" rule.) While I appreciate the need to counsel our children against the violence and aggression of the superheroes, I think superheroes serve a purpose in young children's lives, especially boys', that puts allowing their use in a more positive light.

The overwhelming majority of superhero storytellers are boys. I believe that young boys tell superhero stories for the same reason they are drawn to them: because they are well aware of their own inability to protect themselves from real danger, and superhero stories play out their triumph over the aggression they perceive in our culture. It is my experience that little boys must learn to manage these powerful figures or they will be managed by them. While obviously our classrooms should not encourage violent behavior, they can offer us an opportunity to discover the things that frighten our children. Also, by tolerating the presence of superheroes and the feelings they stir up in the children's stories, we equate writing and control. In time, when the children have explored these issues satisfactorily, they will use writing to explore other ideas and feelings.

This is not to say that young girls do not have fears or aggressive feelings, simply that girls are not identified with violence in our culture the way that boys are. While our young boys are wearing "Rude Dog" T-shirts, our young girls are wearing "101 Dalmatians" ones. Girls also have their own versions of superheroes, though they are not usually recognized as such. Barbie and My Little Pony and the Little Mermaid all offer stereotypical versions of femaleness that little girls must explore and understand, if they are to be free of their constraints. Most teachers dislike these stories just as much as the boys' superhero stories, since they're just as repetitious and uncreative.

Paley offers another reason why children are so drawn to the superhero theme: "The stories do not reflect the qualities of a particular child or encourage variations. If the child's name is omitted from a superhero story, the authorship is unrecognizable. This must be the point then, I decided. *Such stories are used to mask, not reveal, individuality.*"[1] I find this an extraordinary insight into the world of young children. Contrary to adult perceptions, relationships among classmates are rarely casual at the primary or the pre-school level. Young children continually show and tell us how difficult it is to maintain one's individuality in a group. What teacher of two-year-olds, for example, hasn't marveled at the "monkey-see, monkey-do" effect? What teacher of four- and five-year-olds hasn't had to put a stop to endless discussions of who will come to whose birthday party? And what teacher of seven-year-olds hasn't seen the hesitation in a second grader's eyes as he or she attempts to second-guess the group in a class vote? It's possible that the first step towards being able to differentiate oneself from the group begins in these early years when children spend so much energy coming to grips with the group. Perhaps we should not view their early attempts, including their repetitious and unoriginal stories, as a loss of individuality, but in a sense the preservation of their individuality beneath—as Paley says—"the mask."

The story topics children choose will reveal as much about their developmental phase and sense of self as the skill with which they tell the story. This is not to say all topics should be tolerated. (I, personally, say no to what I call "bathroom" stories that pop up occasionally among immature four-year-olds and some unhappy older kids.) But, for the most part, I think we should censor children's choices of story topics with as light a touch as possible.

🌟 Between Teacher and Child

Over the course of my first year taking down stories, the children's responses to dictation helped me to realize that for non-readers and writers, literacy is not a product but an *interaction*, something that happens, as it was clearly happening for Colin on the day he watched me writing down Miko's story. Most exciting of all to me, dictation proved not to be the province of just so-called successful students—as Miko was sure to be—but of all children, including Colin.

In my first few years in the classroom, preparing children to be literate, teaching "reading readiness," or reading itself was a chore. Children's dictation provided me with an opportunity to discover that teaching reading and writing wasn't a professional obligation, it was part of life. At times, I felt like a parent or caretaker, because it felt so much more natural. After I started taking dictation, I realized that I had never before really listened to them as they participated in reading and writing activities because I had known all the answers. Now, I had only questions, which were tools for the children to use: "What happened after Darth Vader came?" or "Where did the puppy go again?" The open-ended quality of dictation activity is one key to its success.

A child's developmental level is an important factor in his or her ability to tell a story that will set the tone of the interaction between teacher and child. As an example, here are stories by two children from similar backgrounds who exemplify the beginning and mature stages of dictation abilities. Michael was two and Lisa was six. Michael's parents, like Lisa's, read to him frequently at home, but he had never been asked to *tell* a story. In all probability he had no concept of story beyond what he found in picture books. On storytelling day, his teacher, Ms. Bentsen, asked, "Would you like to come to the table and tell me a story?" Michael looked down at the small vinyl horses he held in his hand. He had been carrying them around since early morning, typical behavior for a two-and-a-half-year-old. "Maybe you could tell me about your horses," Ms. Bentsen suggested. Michael walked in the direction of the storytelling table. Through an exchange of questions and answers between him and his teacher, his story evolved:

Michael's Story   *October 12*

These horsies are looking for hay. They're eating it. The palomino got out! The horse got out. The palomino jumped out! Real high!

In another school, Lisa, a kindergartner and an old hand at story dictation, had checked the "storytelling list" earlier that day and found that her turn was next. No sooner had the teacher picked up her pencil than Lisa began:

Lisa's Story   *October 12*

One night a girl named Jessica read a story. And went to sleep. She didn't hear a Ho-Ho-Ho sound or tiny reindeer prancing on her roof. As you all know the person who says Ho-Ho-Ho is Santa. Santa slid down the chimney and went into the living room. He put some toys under the tree and near the fireplace. Jessica woke up on Christmas morning and asked her parents who had come. The parents said, "Santa. You don't know about him?" "No," said Jessica. And she ate breakfast and she waited for her brother Charlie. Then Charlie ate breakfast and asked Jessica, "Will you read my name on all the presents that I got?" "Well," said Jessica, "only if you let me play with you." "Okay," said Charlie. Then Jessica and Charlie opened presents. The End.

As I observed these two children dictating their stories to their respective teachers, I was, as always, intrigued by the nature of the exchange between teacher and child. The child would speak, the teacher would listen, ask a question or two, comment perhaps ("You like those horses, don't you, Mike?" or "Christmas will be coming soon, won't it?"). Then the teacher would write down what the child said. There was something about the reciprocal, give-and-take quality of the relation between teacher and child that has never ceased to fascinate me. Dictation almost always feels cozy and intimate for the teacher and child, a remarkable achievement in a room full of noisy children. I felt this even more keenly when recently I watched two students, Brittany and Althea, each tell a story to Mrs. Thompson, their kindergarten teacher.

Brittany's physical behavior was typical of five-year-olds well acquainted with stories and the dictation process, as well as that of children close to deciphering the world of print on their own. She leaned her upper body over the top of the table as she told her story, her eyes fixed on the point of Mrs. Thompson's pen. She followed the pen across the paper, as it brought her story to life through the printed words. Her teacher's arm was a substitute for her own. Mrs. Thompson welcomed Brittany's interest in the written story, occasionally pointing to a word with her finger, or pausing to let Brittany explore her thoughts a little more.

Brittany's classmate, Althea, who was equally bright, was not as well acquainted with stories or writing as Brittany when she entered kindergarten. Though Althea, too, had been dictating stories for several months, she was still more interested in the opportunity to tell a story than in the printed words. As Althea told her story, she watched Mrs. Thompson's face, taking her cues from the teacher's approving smiles or puzzled looks. I could see that Althea was very much a child who was learning through the love of this teacher's attention, and every inch of her small frame was responding to the sheer delight in that attention. Mrs. Thompson told me later that whereas she had been content to let Althea merely tell her the story at the beginning of the year, she now demanded more thought from Althea before writing it down. Because of her love for her teacher, Althea complied with Mrs. Thompson's inquiries for details about her characters and plot, and her requests to consider the proper tenses of the verbs. When Althea had finished dictating her story, Mrs. Thompson read it from the beginning, calling Althea's attention to the words as she went along. In this instance, Althea's behavior more closely resembled Brittany's; it was a good beginning; she really had progressed.

Mrs. Thompson and Althea's relationship is reminiscent of Jerome Bruner's description of mothers who, probably unconsciously, teach their children in this way by subtly "upping the ante." A mother may tie her children's shoes, or button their coats, or find their favorite toys upon request, for what seems like years on end. Then, one day, without warning, she suggests that the child do it himself, and he does. In the same way, not content to let Althea rest on her laurels of simply discovering storytelling, Mrs. Thompson was asking Althea to exert a little more control over the storytelling and the language.

❧ How "Natural" Is Storytelling?

We think of young children as natural storytellers. "Teacher," two-and-a-half-year-old Melissa calls from the housekeeping corner, "tomorrow is my birthday. And I'm going to invite Katherine to my party." The teacher smiles and tells Melissa that she's sure they will both have a good time. She doesn't mention the fact that Melissa's birthday is not for several months, or that tomorrow is a regular school day. In a kindergarten classroom, five-year-old Amber announces that her sister had to wear rags to the party because her stepmother wouldn't give her any money for new clothes. "Is that so? That reminds me of the Cinderella story we have been reading," her amused teacher answers. Amber nods her head vigorously and returns to her school work. Four-year-old Brad blurts out, "Last year I went Trick or Treating by myself." "Is that true?" a classmate questions, doubtful that a three-year-old would be allowed to wander outside at night. Brad's mouth puckers; he draws himself up straight in his seat. "Yes!" he insists. In fact, it is not true, which he later admits when asked by an adult if he is "sure."

These scenes remind us that young children seem to have a natural ability to tell stories. If what young children tell us is not true, we reason (and we rule out the possibility of lying, which is a very different developmental issue) that it must be a story. What is more interesting here is that children who seem to be natural storytellers do not perceive themselves as storytellers. In response to the questions, "Would you like to tell me a story?" or "Do you have a story to tell?" it is not unusual for children from two to eight to give a blank—and sometimes anxious—stare, even when a moment ago they had seemed excited about the prospect of telling a story. Four-and-a-half-year-old Andrew, for example, was desperate to tell me his first story. He pestered me for a chance until, finally, his name came up on the class rotation list. "What is the story you would like to tell me, Andrew?" I asked, pencil poised over the paper. "A Christmas story!" Andrew crowed. I waited. Andrew's smiling face began to change. He looked perplexed, and stared at the blank paper. "What are the words to your Christmas story, Andrew?" I prodded. "I'll write them here." He looked pensive, eager to cooperate. Finally, he blurted out unhappily, "It is Jingle Bells. The End."

Matthew was a pre-kindergartener who also wanted very much to tell a story for the first time. Unfortunately, he was fourth in line. When I was finally able to give him a turn, I asked, "What are the words to your story?" There was a long silence. "I don't know," Matthew finally answered. "Well," I began slowly, not wanting to push him, "do you want to think about it, and come back to me later?" "I don't know," he said again, though he made no attempt to leave. I offered to get him started: "Do you want to tell me about your family or your new car?" "I don't know," he said again, still not moving. I waited. Finally, he offered, "I have a brother." (Rochelle, his classmate, had told a story about her brother earlier that day.) "Should I write that down?" I asked. He nodded. (It was no coincidence that in this pre-k room, "home" stories—that is, stories of mothers, fathers, and siblings—were the dominant theme.) The next time Matthew came to the storytelling table he was ready: "One day my brother and I. . . ." Matthew finished his story easily this time, but I suspect that, like Andrew above, he probably wasn't telling the original story he had in his mind. It would take a good deal of practice before he could consciously let the words and images flow.

When most young children are asked for the first time "Would you like to tell me a story?", they almost always say yes, but also probably misunderstand the question. They hear the word *story*, and automatically want to participate in whatever it is, but miss the significance of the "tell me" part, because it doesn't fit into their experience. When they are confronted with the teacher's poised pen, they suddenly become aware of the obligation to do something, and not knowing what to do, either fall silent or find only a few words to express the bountiful images in their heads.

❦ The Value of Dictation

Ken Goodman, in his book *What's Whole in Whole Language*, advocates using dictation whenever a child isn't willing to write on his or her own. Many educators still harbor doubts about the educational value of dictating and telling stories, however, and the fact is that dictation has fallen into disfavor in current reading and writing theory. Some Whole Language proponents and writing experts have spoken against it more recently. The following excerpt from *The Whole Language Kindergarten* is a case in point:

> After examining the research data describing young children's writing (Clay, 1975) and research on the writing process (Graves, 1983), Kathy also decided to make some changes in the way she helped the children become writers. She recognized that, in the dictation process, when she wrote captions and stories for the children, she did not allow the children to use their own knowledge of how print works. . . . She planned instead to encourage children to form their own letters and to use their own invented spellings to write captions for the pictures they drew, as well as *to write longer messages and stories.* [2]

Dictation needs to be rescued from this maligned position for the simple reason that dictation, at least in the form of dictating stories, is *not yet about writing* per se. It's about developing a *relationship* to stories, it's about what's inside. What young children know, feel, and want to say is far more sophisticated than either their knowledge of writing or their physical ability to write it down. In telling their stories to a teacher, young children develop a relationship to their own stories as well as a relationship to print. Both are necessary precursors of writing. Far too many young children are challenged "to be a writer" in some Whole Language or writing process classrooms before they have discovered what they really want to say, or how to say it. Dictation gives them a chance to do this. Without dictation, I would not have realized that Colin, the young boy in my kindergarten class who had been labeled Educable Mentally Handicapped and was performing well below grade level, was a child with a story, and what that story was.

Dictation is a wonderful way to develop children's storytelling abilities because it can be adjusted to the maturity of the teller. "You just tell me the words you would like me to write on the paper, and I'll write them down" will receive any number of responses, given the child's experience with storytelling. For kids who are really stuck, or who need a less open-ended beginning, a more suggestive comment from the teacher might begin, "Well, sometimes stories begin 'Once upon a time.' Would you like to begin your story that way?" This is usually welcome advice to the novice storyteller. Experienced young storytellers often start their stories with "Once upon a time" even before they have sat down. Furthermore, dictation is practical because it allows for a considerable amount of learning and teaching in a relatively short period of time.

🌾 *Dramatization after Dictation*

Dictation is not a revolutionary idea in early childhood education. It's been around long enough to fall into disfavor and, as Paley writes, it wasn't always popular with the children themselves:

> Story dictation had been a minor activity in my previous kindergartens, even though books and dramatics had been high-priority activities. Few children chose to tell a story if they could do something else instead. For years I accepted the "fact" that no more than four or five children out of twenty-five enjoyed dictating stories, and most often they were girls.[3]

Teachers who read *Wally's Stories* often report having similar experiences. I know I did. Something about the dictation process fails to appeal to most young children. What revitalized the idea of dictation was Paley's notion of using dictation intensively, *coupled with acting out the stories at Circle or*

Group Time. Paley noted that regularly doing these two activities together could result in changes in classroom life that are sometimes startling.

The success of the dictation activity, therefore, relies on the promise of dramatization. Without the second, the potential of the first will not be fulfilled:

> Before, we had never acted out these stories. We had dramatized every other kind of printed word—fairy tales, story books, poems, songs—but it had always seemed enough just to write the children's words. Obviously it was not; the words did not sufficiently represent the action, which needed to be shared. For this alone, the children would give up play time, as it was a true extension of play.[4]

Paley's discovery tells us a great deal about how young children view the printed word, especially words without pictures. Clearly, writing stories does not appeal on its own merits, not yet anyway.

Young children's interest in a concrete representation of their stories (the drama or "action") coincides with young children's emotional need to establish their individual identity within the group. Despite our image of young children as egocentric, and our desire for them to act independently, young children can be intensely involved with each other, at least when they're working out social relations. ("Teacher, Joshua won't play with me." "If you don't give me a turn, you can't come to my birthday party.") Paley says that acting out stories in the classroom helps answer "one of the children's most important questions: what do other children think about?"[5]

It is also very clear that children are drawn to dramatization because it provides a guaranteed opportunity to exercise some control over the class for the few minutes it takes to act out each author's story. In other words, children are drawn to the dramatization activity for the same reason they are drawn to other forms of sociodramatic play: to exercise some control over their lives, their wishes, and their destinies. Surely, we have all heard of young children attempting to control play in the block corner, in the library area, on line for the bathroom, on the playground. Dramatization offers the child-author an opportunity to have the final say in a play situation, irresistible for most children. If classroom rules allow the author of the story to choose the cast, this furthers his or her influence over the action (although, as Paley points out, this isn't absolutely necessary, and teachers should feel free to experiment). The dramatization activity, therefore, beyond any literary or literacy pretensions, presents a lesson in social interactions for the child. The dramatization of two-and-a-half-year old Michael's story illustrates what this might look like in its earliest stages:

TEACHER: Michael's story is about his horses. It goes like this: "These horsies are looking for hay. They're eating it. The palomino got out! The horse got out. The palomino jumped out! Real high!" Michael, which horse do you want to be in the play?

MICHAEL: The palomino.

TEACHER: Choose someone to be the other horse who eats hay with you.

[Michael chooses William.]

TEACHER: William, will you be a horse in Michael's play?

[William nods "yes."]

TEACHER: Okay. Now, Michael and William get on the stage.

[Michael and William stand in the center of the circle.]

TEACHER: Can you boys pretend to be horses looking for hay? Good. "The palomino gets out!"

[Michael jumps up.]

TEACHER: "The horse got out."

[William jumps up.]

TEACHER: "The palomino jumped out. Real high!"

[Michael jumps again.]

TEACHER: Good acting. You boys looked just like horses jumping.

[Michael and William grin and sit down.]

Since dramatization requires a story to dramatize, it creates a natural need in the children to dictate a story, and hence, brings us full circle.

❧ School Success and Beyond

Current research in literacy development tells us that children who are familiar with print from an early age have an easier time with formal reading instruction, including a greater sense of confidence in their potential to read.[6] We also know that even first and second graders, so-called beginning readers, continue to respond best to reading and writing experiences that arise out of real classroom needs and experiences. If this is the true goal of our reading and writing curriculum, then certainly the dictation and dramatization activities described here offer a valuable means to this end.

The wonderful thing about dictation and dramatization activities, however, is that they teach our children much more than just how to succeed at school. Children who tell stories and act them out—whether they're two and a half or three or seven or eight years old—are learning to *empower* themselves in their world through self-knowledge as well as social knowledge. Through telling their own stories, little children can learn to defend themselves, psychologically speaking, against dragons and monsters, bad guys and burglars, sibling rivalry and conformity. As the sample stories in appendix A demonstrate, these very young authors have found a way to *become* the much admired Ninja turtle or big sister, at least temporarily, which may be long enough. How did they do it? Through the combination of print and action, not for its own sake, as in a basal reader, but for the sake of life's issues, just like real authors and real readers. To be literate is, first and foremost, to manipulate symbols in one's world so as to understand that world. It is my experience that a classroom in which young children dictate and dramatize their own stories is a classroom of mythmakers who become, in the process, problem solvers. In doing so, they are actively combining two distinct, but equally important, educational goals. This, in turn, assists the children's ego development, and we come full circle once again.

Placing dictation and dramatization activities at the heart of the curriculum can offer us knowledge about the children we teach, knowledge we need in order to teach humanely. As Robert Coles writes in *The Call of Stories*:

> The people who come to see us bring us their stories. They hope they tell them well enough so that we understand the truth of their lives. They hope we know how to interpret their stories correctly. We have to remember that what we hear is *their story.*[7]

What better place to begin to teach reading and writing than with what children want to know about: themselves?

---

1. Paley, Vivian, *Wally's Stories*, p. 129.
2. Raines and Canady, *The Whole Language Kindergarten*, p. 25.
3. Paley, Vivian, *Wally's Stories*, p. 10.
4. Ibid., p. 12.
5. Ibid., p. 66.
6. Strickland and Morrow, eds. *Emerging Literacy*, p. 31.
7. Coles, Robert, *The Call of Stories*, p. 7.

Chapter Five

❉

PORTRAITS OF
YOUNG STORYTELLERS

Eric finished his sentence, and looked at the paper on which his teacher had been writing down his story.
"Is that it?" he asked.
"Do you mean are you finished?" his teacher said, responding to his obvious confusion as to where the words on the paper had come from. "I don't know. It's your story."
Eric smiled.

—From a pre-kindergarten classroom

Teachers report that, to some five-year-olds, telling stories is second nature, while some eight-year-olds appear defeated before they've begun. It is clear that age alone does not make a writer, nor is dictating or writing a benefit merely of having learned to read. In order to competently—and confidently—"write a story," children must have some understanding of the writing process itself. As I have pointed out, the regular opportunity to dictate stories can be an enormous aid to this understanding. The question now is: What can teachers learn about writing from children who dictate stories? Over the years, many teachers and I have studied young children's behavior as they dictated stories. We have listened carefully to children's words, and have monitored whether they tell their stories in conversational tones, oblivious of the dictation process, or whether they adopt a more formal tone, as in true dictation. We have studied whether their eyes actually follow the script or drift around the room as they speak. We have watched how young children squirm in their seats or sit calmly as they dictate their stories, and more. We have come to conclude that children's progress as storytellers follows relatively similar patterns that, for the most part, help us identify where the children stand in their progress towards independent writing.

For example, it turns out that Colin, the little boy from my first kindergarten class who was labeled Educable Mentally Handicapped, was not at all unusual when he fixed on my pencil point and the print that seemed to stream from it as I wrote. Many kids in the stage between pre-writing and writing are shocked by the realization that the words that flow from the teacher's pencil are the same as those the child just said. In fact, the teachers and I have identified several key stages in the storyteller's behavior leading up to the point where independent story writing is a reasonable expectation. We were not surprised to discover that after the age of four or five, the types of behavior we observed almost always correspond not with a given child's age, but with his or her previous experience with both stories and writing.

In brief, we found that in children who dictate stories regularly there are roughly three stages of development, which approximate pre-writing, "almost" writing, and ready-to-write stages. In addition, each stage can be described by three criteria: 1) control over language when telling a story; 2) awareness of writing as a tool to capture thoughts or oral communication; and 3) physical behavior when telling a story.

I'd like to explore these observations of stages of development in young children's stories in more detail for the simple reason that they have been so very helpful to teachers in appreciating what a very long road children must travel to become independent writers. By doing so, we stand a better chance of tailoring their early reading and writing curriculum to their needs.

𝕩 *Stages in Dictation*

Stage 1: Pre-writing

New storytellers can be as young as two. Of course, they also can be much older. Some older children with previous experience with stories and storytelling may skip this stage entirely. Not all children go through the first stage in dictating stories.

Control of language. Essentially, for the very young, storytelling is associated with talking. First stories may not contain any sentences, however, but merely isolated words that come to mind randomly or refer to objects in the classroom that the storyteller happens to see. For example, Julia's first story, at the age of twenty-five months, was "Baby. Book," taken from her housekeeping play moments before. Four-and-a-half-year-old Jared dictated this story to his teacher: "Shoe. Motorcycle. Pencil. Block," a list of objects from his classroom. Newcomers to storytelling who are a little older might offer a whole sentence or more, but the stories are often not representative of the child's linguistic sophistication in normal circumstances.

Awareness of writing. From a cognitive perspective, storytellers in the first stage of dictation are often unaware of the relationship between what they are saying and what the teacher is writing down. The finished product is, therefore, unintentional, and even serendipitous. Later on, during the dramatization process, novice storytellers often seem pleasantly surprised that the teacher has a piece of paper with the same words on it that they had told her earlier. Clearly, these children are in the earliest stages of relating to print. Very young children also don't understand that one of the primary functions of the teacher's role as scribe is to echo the children's words verbatim—this, after all, is pretty unusual behavior in grown-ups. My experience with three-year-old Sean and his misunderstanding of this is typical. Sean's story began, "I went to the store." I then echoed his words as I wrote them down—"I went to the store." Sean paused in his storytelling, looked up with a curious expression, and asked, "You, too?"

Physical behavior. The physical behavior of novice storytellers is also significant. For one, they rarely position themselves for the role. Instead of sitting in the chair, ready to talk, they half-sit, they stand, they come, they go. Sometimes they can't resist the urge to write as the teacher writes, and they insist on their own paper and pencil. They are not really mimicking the teacher's actions here, but merely joining her. Novice storytellers who do sit calmly from the start are motivated, more often than not, by the opportunity for special attention from the teacher, and not simply by the opportunity to tell a story.

In content, first-stage stories range from the mundane to the fantastic. They can almost always be directly traced to some experience or idea the child has had or is trying to make sense of. Although the very youngest storytellers will tell things that are not true, strictly speaking, they are not "making things up" for the sake of the story, but rather thinking imaginatively, as is developmentally appropriate for this age.

Stage 2: Almost Writing

Control of language. In the second stage, young storytellers have begun to control the language the scribe writes down. Storytellers will now frequently speak in sentences, though the sentences might not form a coherent whole. Often second-stage storytellers are satisfied with simple references to themselves, family life, and events that, in part, are based in reality. Stories at this stage often receive credit for being better than they are because the teacher's personal knowledge of the children will give added meaning to some rather sparse prose.

Awareness of writing. The storyteller in the second stage has made a leap in his or her understanding of writing as separate from drawing. "This is for you," said two-and-a-half-year-old Dylan, thrusting a torn piece of paper at me, covered with scribbles. "I wrote it." Beginning storytellers are grappling with rules that govern print on the page. For example, four-year-old Jason thought that his name would fit "in there," pointing to a space between paragraphs, "because it's a short name and short names fit in small spaces." Storytellers at this stage may still let the scribe take full responsibility for the actual writing, and tell their stories to the air, almost as soliloquies. Later, many will put their noses to the page, acting as if they must monitor the process to make sure the scribe is getting it right. Some children dictate very quickly, unaware that writing is slower than talking. At some point, when they grasp what the scribe is actually doing, most children will slow down, waiting for each word to appear on the page before they can say the next one. ("We . . . saw . . . little . . . houses. . . .")

It is important for all teachers of young children, but especially primary grade teachers whose children have a higher degree of writing ability, to understand the great variance in children's awareness of written speech. Before children can be expected to write their own stories, they should have plenty of opportunities to observe the rhythm of writing down speech. Writing what one thinks is a learned, not a natural skill.

Physical behavior. The storyteller's physical behavior in this second stage has advanced greatly from the first. The child comes to the storytelling table ready to act like a storyteller, waiting for the moment to begin. Storytellers

in this stage still use their bodies as much as their minds, squirming in their seats and leaning into the desk. In the course of taking down a one-page story, I observed five-year-old Kelly move back and forth between two seats no fewer than fourteen times! After that I stopped counting. They also change their voices to suit their meaning: "Once and FOR ALL!"

The content of students' stories at this stage varies widely. Often the children recount stories of their home lives, which we call "home stories." Superhero stories, especially among boys, are also quite prevalent. It is not unusual for a single theme to come to dominate the stories in a classroom; often this theme can be traced back to the first or second story that was ever told and dramatized in the class. (See "Borrowing" in chapter 4.)

Stage 3: Ready to Write

Control of language. In the third stage of becoming a storyteller, children exhibit a fuller sense of story: they come to the storytelling table with ideas to fashion into a story; they are aware of the written page as a representation of their ideas; and they see the scribe now as mere medium. (In turn, at this stage, the scribe has little difficulty in grasping the storyteller's intentions.)

Awareness of writing. By this stage, the storyteller's ideas are usually clear and logical. Children in this stage have adopted the formal language of storytelling: they are comfortable with conventions such as "Once upon a time . . ." or "In the meantime. . . ." Now the storyteller takes possession of the print to point out a mistake or interesting idea. ("You messed that up," Jude said, referring to his teacher's misspelling of a word he had said. Joyce pointed to the page and asked her teacher, "Does that say *popsicle*? And that? And that?")

Physical behavior. Physically, the young storytellers have settled down in their chairs. They tell their stories efficiently and effortlessly. The content of their stories may still be oriented toward superheroes, but they are more willing to branch out, especially if stimulated by a new book, movie, or another child's ideas.

At this point, typically between six and eight years old, children begin trying to write down their own stories, though they still write quite slowly. The mind is faster than the hand, which can be frustrating to an experienced storyteller. But this is quite natural: just as we wouldn't expect first and second graders to walk the same distance as their middle school brothers and sisters, we should not expect them to write as much. For this reason, teachers should continue to offer dictation to these advanced storytellers, along with the clear expectation they also write on their own. Teachers who are careful observers of their children will know, like parents, when to up the ante by asking a child to write on his or her own.

❊ Stages in Dramatization

Children's ability to act out stories is a further indication of their growth as storytellers. Dramatization is also a boost to story writing because, in most classrooms, children have more opportunities to act in a story than to write one, giving them added practice in focusing on the precise meaning of words. In fact, teachers often find that children's acting abilities may exceed their storytelling development, at least for a time. Furthermore, the social nature of the dramatization helps children work through their ideas about stories and acting, an added boost for learning about stories.

Young children know about pretending from many sources: from their own play, from previous dramatic productions at school, and, for those old enough to grapple with the mystery of it, the distinction between real life and television. When it comes to dramatizing stories without props or rehearsals, they learn very quickly at all ages. The three stages in dramatization generally reflect a child's ability to act out the meaning of the words with a greater and greater precision.

Stage 1

When toddlers first act out stories, they need a lot of prompting. If the story reads, "Alligator bite me. He beat me all up. Him bite Mrs. Simmons. Him bite Matthew," the child's teacher may have to ask the child playing the alligator, "Can you show us what an alligator looks like when he tries to bite someone?" To the child playing Mrs. Simmons, the teacher might have to say, "What would you do if an alligator bit you?" The teacher would then wait for the child to act on her questions. Toddlers and young nursery school children who are newcomers to dramatization will need some more prompting, such as "Maybe you can open up your mouth very wide, like an alligator," or "Are you an alligator that stands up?" (They never are. This prompt always sends little ones

down on all fours.) Older children, even those with little experience acting out such stories, without rehearsal or props, catch on quickly.

Stage 2

The second stage in dramatization comes when the children are ready for
more subjective suggestions regarding the intentions or feelings behind the
words, as well as more precise actions. For instance, the teacher might ask,
"It says here that you got lost in the woods. Did that make you scared?
Can you show us?" Likewise, the teacher might focus on the action more
specifically. Regarding a dinner scene, the teacher might ask, "Do you eat
with your hands or do you use forks and spoons?" If the class is dramatizing a story about going on a trip, it will often raise an inquiry about
who's driving. The teacher can ask, "Did everyone drive the car, or just
one person? The mommy? Where did the children sit?" Sometimes the
teacher will want to direct her questions to the author, while other questions may be more appropriate for another child—or all the children.

The idea here is for the teacher, without intruding too much on the
drama, to help the actors interpret the author's intentions as accurately as
possible. It is a delicate balancing act, but one that's well worth the effort,
since most young authors love the attention their story receives.

Stage 3

The third stage in dramatization occurs at the point when the teacher
begins to talk more for the benefit of the audience than of the actors ("I
like the way you are carefully rocking the baby's cradle. It makes me think
there's a real cradle on the stage."), because the actors have become so
skilled that they no longer need much help.

❧ *Anthropologists in Our Own Classrooms*

Unlike more traditional measures of children's early literacy development,
such as a check-off sheet of basic skills, observation of children's behavior during the dictation and dramatization activities tells us not so much
what children already know about reading and writing, but what they're
in the process of knowing, a substantially more informative measurement
than the first. As a bonus, teachers report that by taking the time to study
carefully young children's behavior dictating and dramatizing stories, they
themselves have the pleasure of being anthropologists in their own class-

rooms. It serves to point out the incredible resource—the children them-selves—that we have before us every day as we strive to be better teachers. For too long, teachers have denied themselves what should be one of the greatest rewards of teaching: the permission to observe what Nancie Atwell calls children "coming to know."

✧

Chapter Six

A Guide to Storytelling in the Classroom

"My kids couldn't do that. Maybe yours. Not mine."

—Teacher of three-year-olds

The step-by-step guide to classroom activities in this chapter offers some practical advice to teachers who might want to try the same ideas in their classrooms. All such advice, of course, must be filtered through the individual teacher's own experience and goals. Just as the methods described in this book are largely my own interpretations of Vivian Paley's work, I wouldn't expect my remarks to be embraced by the reader without modification. Classrooms are living environments that force us to reevaluate all advice in light of the circumstances in front of us at the moment. My intention in this chapter, therefore, is only to offer a starting point for teachers interested in using dictation and dramatization activities with young children.

❧ *The Dictation and Dramatization Activities*

Logistics: What, When, Who, Where, with What

I. *Dictation and Dramatization: Working Definitions*

Dictation is the process in which a child tells his or her story to a scribe, in most cases, a teacher, who writes it down.

Dramatization is the process by which stories are read aloud and then acted out by members of the class usually without rehearsals or props. This includes both adult-authored and child-authored stories. In child-authored stories, the most popular procedure is for the child-author to choose the role he or she would like to play, and then which classmates will play the rest. As the story is read aloud by the teacher, the children perform their parts. Dramatization of adult-authored stories follows the same format, except that the teacher usually assigns the roles.

It is important to note that in order for there to be any impact on the children's early reading and writing development, each child must have *regular* opportunities to dictate and dramatize his or her stories, as well as to dramatize adult-authored stories. What constitutes a regular opportunity is discussed in Sections II–VII.

II. *When in the Daily Schedule Are Stories Dictated?*

The dictation activity requires that the teacher be free to meet with the children individually. Scheduling time for this one-on-one attention is the biggest hurdle in using the dictation activities, and the teacher may have to try a couple of different schedules before finding the right one. (Dramatization happens during Group Time, and therefore is rarely a scheduling problem.)

In a pre-school or kindergarten classroom with two teachers (or one teacher and an assistant), it helps if the second teacher is largely responsible for the rest of the students while dictation is being taken. If a second teacher is not available, you might enlist a parent volunteer or aide. Teachers of older children often prefer working alone. In reality, the teacher/scribe must expect some interruptions from the other children, but this has never seemed an undue problem for the storytellers.

Most teachers prefer to take stories at a time that is not teacher-directed. Free Play or Center Time—when the children are free to move about the room, playing in the different content areas—is most popular with teachers. Kindergarteners and first and second graders usually have less Center Time than pre-schoolers, and some teachers prefer to take dictation when the other children are busy at their desks. While this cuts down on the social interaction around storytelling—and is, in ideal terms, a great loss—the more important thing is that the children have the opportunity to tell their stories.

Let's take two examples of dictation scenes during an unrestricted period of the day. Imagine it's Monday morning at Center Time in a pre-kindergarten classroom. Some children are in the block corner. Some are in the housekeeping area. A couple are at the art table with glue and beads. A few more are pouring purple water through different-sized beakers at the water table. One is in the bathroom. One has come in late and is still eating his snack. Two more are in the book corner. The teacher is sitting at what is called the storytelling table with one child who is dictating a story, while another is waiting her turn.

By contrast, a Houston teacher, Tammy Copeland, has worked dictation into a fairly traditional schedule, which includes reading groups that she works with at the "reading table" Monday through Thursday. On Friday, however, Ms. Copeland calls individual members of only one reading group to the table, giving them the opportunity to tell her a story. By the time the reading groups are usually finished, she has taken five or six stories. In the meantime, all of the other children are busy with the normal activities Ms. Copeland plans for reading group time. The stories are acted out just before lunch, one or two a day, that morning and all the following week. The next Friday, Ms. Copeland calls members from the next reading group, and so forth. This schedule gives each child the opportunity to dictate a story about once a month.

Teachers of children over four should allow for approximately seven to ten minutes per story. Most younger children are finished in a matter of a few minutes.

III. When in the Daily Schedule Are Stories Dramatized?

Stories are usually dramatized later in the morning or afternoon, either before or after a significant transition, such as from Center Time to recess, or from seat work to specialist or lunch. Some teachers prefer to save dramatization for the last period of the day.

IV. How Do Children Get a Chance to Dictate?

Some teachers take stories only from children who ask, but under this system not all children will tell stories, for not all children, especially the very young ones, will remember to ask. Most teachers I work with prefer to ask each child, on a rotating basis, if he or she would like a turn. This reminds them of the opportunity. Generally, teachers keep a class list handy for this purpose, and simply mark off when a child has been asked.

V. How Do Children Get a Chance to Dramatize?

As I have mentioned, most teachers seem to prefer that the child who writes the story choose the part he or she would like to play, and who will play the others. Since it often happens that some children are chosen more often than others, almost all teachers insist that a child may not be asked twice on the same day until everyone in the class has had a chance. Vivian Paley examined this issue in her book *You Can't Say You Can't Play*. She concluded that, in the interest of fairness, all parts should be assigned on a rotating basis. Some teachers feel this would diminish the popularity of the activity, but Paley says this is not the case. I encourage teachers to think about and experiment with this issue, and, along with the children, decide what works best in their rooms.

VI. How Many Times a Week Does Dictation Take Place?

Some teachers prefer to take a few stories every day. Most prefer to take three or four stories two days a week, which frees them up for other special activities on the remaining days. Ideally, children under five should get to tell a story once every two weeks. This is frequent enough for the children to grow in their skill at storytelling, as well as to observe closely the process involved in writing down spoken language. Sometimes, of course, the class is too large for children to have a turn this often.

VII. How Many Times a Week Does Dramatization Take Place?

Ideally, dramatization of children's stories should occur the same day the stories are dictated. Older children usually have little trouble waiting until the end of the day or even a little longer, if the teacher carefully explains what the schedule will be and sticks to it. Three-, four-, and five-year-olds, however, seem to prefer dramatization to take place at least by the end of the morning.

Adult-authored dramatization should occur at least once a week. This allows for the experience of acting out formal language and for far more sophisticated ideas to have a positive impact on children's knowledge of stories.

VIII. Where Does Dictation Take Place?

Dictation can take place anywhere in the classroom. Most teachers prefer a set place that the children come to identify with storytelling. Supplies can be kept there, as another reminder. I prefer a table with two or three chairs, one for me, the storyteller, and possibly a friend or two. I also prefer a view of the whole room, so I usually sit with my back to a wall.

IX. What Supplies Are Needed for Dictation?

The only supplies necessary for these activities are paper (blank or ruled, preferably 8 1/2 by 11 inches), carbon paper, and a pen or pencil.

While the paper and pen are obvious, many teachers wonder about the carbon paper. The carbon paper provides an immediate copy. One is given to the storyteller, and the other copy is kept by the teacher to read aloud during dramatization. This promotes a sense of ownership in the young author, while relieving teachers of the problem of having to retrieve the story from the child for dramatization. Later the teacher can file her copies in a binder of class stories, which for the children underscores their value.

I prefer a special box in which to store the story supplies. Convenient for having everything together, it also acts as a reminder to the children, like the binder of stories, that stories are a part of classroom life.

X. Where Does Dramatization Take Place?

In most classrooms, the children sit in a circle on the floor for dramatization, the interior of which becomes the "stage." In one overcrowded first grade classroom I observed, the space was too cramped to accommodate a group circle. The teacher simply arranged the desks in such a way that everyone in the audience had a clear view of the front of the room where the dramatization took place.

XI. What Supplies Are Needed for Dramatization?

Because dramatization is an activity that occurs with great frequency in the classroom, and whose primary goal is to share one child's ideas with the rest of the class, props are rarely used and even unnecessary. Occasionally, the children will request something specific, such as the piano footrest for the little bear's chair in a retelling of *The Three Bears*. Teachers should feel free to include props or not, but using them all the time will get burdensome to the teacher, and detracts from the very valuable lesson of imagining the action and scenery ("Can you show us how you would hold a hot cup of cocoa?"). I usually reserve props and costumes for special occasions.

❦ Getting Started

I. Adult-Authored Dramatization or Dictation First?

Most teachers prefer to begin with dramatization of adult-authored stories, maybe two a week for a couple of weeks. This sets the tone for stories as a regular part of classroom life, and also provides an opportunity for children to become familiar with dramatic terminology and with acting without rehearsals or props.

II. Talking with the Children

Teachers should approach the dictation and dramatization activities as they would any change in the curriculum. A day or two before you plan to begin, make an announcement at Circle or Group Time. As always, simple explanations are best: "Tomorrow, we're going to act out *The Three Billy Goats Gruff.*" Establish terminology and basic rules, using familiar terms: "The inside of our circle will be the stage for our play." "Authors" and "actors" and "act out" are some terms you may need to explain. You won't need to explain everything ahead of time, however; during the first couple of dramatizations, opportunities will arise to discuss "dialogue," "offstage," and other dramatic terms.

It is very helpful to establish a No Touching rule for dramatization. This means just what it says. Young children don't always restrain themselves when acting out aggressive behavior. The No Touching rule helps avoid this problem. The No Touching rule is the only hard and fast rule in dramatization. Teachers should remind children of it as often as required. One side benefit is that children extend the rule to other areas of excessively aggressive play.

Many teachers prefer to limit the number of actors to four or five, though there may be other characters in the story that the children can imagine "on stage." This cuts down on potential confusion on stage, and also guarantees a sizable audience.

III. Directing Adult-Authored Stories

Children often have little experience with acting, and will need help coming up with ideas. "Is that the way a troll would look?" "Does the biggest billy goat use his head to push the troll off the bridge?" Ask the audience for suggestions: "Can anyone think of a way to show the billy goats eating grass?"

IV. Talking with the Children about Dictation

After two or more dramatizations of adult-authored stories, teachers can let the children know that they will have a chance now to tell their own stories, which will also be acted out. Teachers will need to help children understand that they will be dictating their stories, and don't need to worry if they can't write yet. Teachers can help the children envision the dictation activity by showing them the materials and where it will take place in the room.

V. Choosing Who Goes First

Usually, teachers choose the first few storytellers based on the expectation that the children will see the activity as fun and be able to tell enough so that the others have an idea what to do when it's their turn. It's best to accept, with a minimum of intervention, whatever the first-time storytellers have to say. The immediate goal is to allow the children to become comfortable with the dictation process as non-judgmental and open-ended. Later, they will be more open to questions and suggestions.

VI. Directing Child-Authored Dramas

Dramatization of children's stories does not differ significantly from that of adult-authored stories. The one exception, of course, is that the teacher can ask the author to clarify puzzling or ambiguous parts. The teacher might comment, "When you say, 'Then we drove home,' who should sit in the driver's seat?" or "Did everyone come to the party, or just the children?" The teacher might make a suggestion to lend more excitement or feeling to the action: "Is the boy glad to find his puppy?" or "Did Shredder make Donatello angry?"

❦ The Role of the Teacher / Scribe

In the dictation activity, the teacher acts as a scribe, whose primary job is to write down what the child says. Usually, she echoes the child's words as she writes, both to keep the child on track and to make sure she's hearing correctly. In the event that the teacher does not understand something the child says, or does not follow the child's line of reasoning, or wishes to move the story along, she may question the child. These questions and their answers should result in a conversation between two interested parties, as well as a type of internal editing associated with the writing process. Essentially, we are asking the children to consider questions that they will eventually learn to ask themselves when making up or revising a story unassisted.

The teacher's questions or responses below are not chiseled in stone, nor are they complete. Some child somewhere will say something that will force us to create new ones.

I. Basic Types of Responses

A. *Story initiation* These questions simply get the ball rolling: "What's your story about today?" "How does your story begin?" "I'm ready now. You may begin."

B. *Echoing as you write* As the child dictates his story, the scribe echoes his words while writing them down.

C. *Echoing as you write, with modification* Scribe changes some words, usually for grammatical correctness.

D. *Rereading what the child has said so far* Sometimes children can't think of what to say next. Rereading what was said up to that point can sometimes give them a new idea.

E. *Redirection* Very young children often need to be refocused on the story. Scribe might say, "Yes, there's Danny. You can play with him when you're finished telling me your story. Is there more you want to tell me about the airplane?"

F. *Cue to proceed* Scribe indicates that the child may continue. "Okay" or "Yes?" or "Then what happened?"

G. *Monitoring speed* Scribe asks the child to speed up or slow down.

H. *Reiteration*	Scribe repeats what the child says without writing it down to ask if she has heard the words correctly. She might add something akin to "Is that what you said?"
I. *Reiteration with modification*	Without writing it down, scribe repeats, with some modification, what the child says. She might add, "Is that what you're trying to tell me?"
J. *Considering grammar*	Many teachers welcome the opportunity to model standard English for their students. "Do you mean to say 'goed' or 'went'?" or "Should I put 'They was at home' or 'They were at home'?" When young children are not interested in choosing the standard version, it usually means they don't hear the problem. Correcting it, therefore, has no real educational value.

Considering grammar can be a delicate issue when the speaker does not come from a home where standard English is spoken. Most teachers prefer to offer children the choice anyway. A "correct" answer should never be mandatory, however.

The important thing to keep in mind is that the goal is story writing, not perfect English. There is plenty of time for that when the children are older and more confident of their story writing abilities.

K. *Distinction between general ideas and actual story line*	A child may run on for several sentences without making it clear whether he or she is actually telling the story or just thinking about it aloud. The scribe can ask, "Do you want me to write all those words?" or "So, should I write . . . ?" It is very important that the scribe avoid a comment such as "How should I write that?" even though this is a very natural way

to phrase the question—it often makes children think that what they just said wasn't acceptable.

L. *Story conclusion*   "We're almost at the end of the page now. Can you think of a way to end your story?" or "Do you want your story to end on this page, or do you want to continue it the next time you have a chance to tell a story?"

II. Beyond Basics: Shaping the Story

A. *Asking the child to reflect on his or her story in different ways*

1) More information needed: "Who is that? You haven't mentioned him before." or "Let's stop here a moment. What happened to the mommy?"

2) Finding the logic: "I don't understand. How did the children escape from the witch?" or "I thought it was bedtime. Why are they eating breakfast?" or "You said the ghosts were all gone. Where did this ghost come from?"

3) Expanding on the stated events: "Why was the mother crying?" or "Do you want to tell me what the children did when they saw the monster?"

4) Expanding on the implied feelings: "I wonder why the little girl was so sad" or "Was the little boy excited when he rode in the plane?"

B. *Asides*   Scribe indicates her approval of the child's ideas with comments that show interest, pleasure, surprise. Scribes should be specific in their comments: "Oh, what a great idea it is to have the car turn into a boat" or "I like the part where the puppy comes home."

C. Rereading the story for the whole picture or to introduce the possibility of changes	Scribe rereads the entire story to help the child form a coherent sense of the whole, which is often not present at this level of storytelling. Rereading the story also offers the teacher the opportunity to introduce revision. Asking "Is there anything you want to change?" is an especially helpful hint that tells the author he or she is in charge of the language and the story, an important realization for the novice storyteller.

III. The List

Teachers invariably report that after the first few dramatizations, the children are lining up for a turn to dictate a story. It helps to make a list and to check off the name of the child who told a story on a given day so that both teacher and children can immediately see whose turn comes next. Referring to the list also helps demonstrate the usefulness of reading and writing.

🌑 *Be Critical and Patient*

Again, the strategies suggested here are only suggestions from teachers and my own observations of young children dictating and dramatizing stories. Each teacher should view her children's participation in the activities with a critical eye, asking herself what strategies seemed to work best, or worst, and why. It takes a while for teachers to feel comfortable with dictation and dramatization. Like all challenging teaching opportunities, these are ideas to grow into, rather than master. Most of the teachers who use dictation and dramatization report that the real payoff takes six months to a year. But all of them report that it's worth waiting for. Good luck!

Sample Stories Dictated to Teachers

The following stories suggest the diversity of young children's storytelling interests and abilities. The children dictated all of these stories with the understanding that they would be acted out.

Toddlers (first-time storytellers)

Ellen
Two years, five months

My summer.
Swimming.
A swimsuit.
It's got Mickey on it!
My grandpa.
My grandma.
I'm going to visit them. I'm going to go on an airplane.
The End.

★ ★ ★

Rachel
Two years, two months

My Katie!
Went to Astroworld.
The End.

Kindergarteners (first-time storytellers)

Helene
Five years, three months

Fire floated everywhere in the house.
The firemen came to take out the fire.
And the firemen saved somebody in the house.

★ ★ ★

Aiesha
Five years, eleven months

My story is Spiderman was swinging on his web.
The End.

★ ★ ★

Justin
Five years, eleven months

It's about fire.
At my uncle's house. I lighted up a match but it didn't lighted and I
hurt my finger.
It's a true story.
Nobody watched me.
My parents was watching TV, even my uncle.
That's all.
Even my sisters.

★ ★ ★

Julia
Five years, eight months

There was a fire. In the kitchen. In the stove. The firemen came out
to blow it out.
The End.

★ ★ ★

Chris
Six years, ten months

I had a fire in my house and the firemen came. My mommy called
them.
The End.

Superhero Stories

Brett
Five years, six months

The Teenage Mutant Ninja Turtle Movie

One day there were crimes all over the city. April O'Neal, crime re-
porter, talked on her microphone. And one of the footsoldiers put his
hand over her mouth. And then the sewer lid opened. There was one
green hand. Then he threw slime at him. He took April O'Neal into
the sewer. And Michelangelo, Donatello, and Leonardo said, "Why
did you bring her here?" Michelangelo ordered a pizza. The pizza man
said, "What the ???" Michelangelo said, "You are two minutes late,
dude." Then the footsoldiers came to the hiding place. And they
fighted the turtles. Then Raphael came flying into the window. One
of the footsoldiers spit water at Leonardo. The End.

★ ★ ★

Mark
Five years, eight months

Sky Turtles

One day Michelangelo was eating pizza on a scale. And then Donatello
said, "One more pizza with chocolate sprinkles and you are going to
have to let out your shell!" They went out the sewers and drive in the
turtle van. Then Michelangelo said, "Scope out the street up ahead."
Then the turtle van fell upside down. Then Rock Steady and Bebop
and two footsoldiers came. And then Bebop, Rock Steady, and the
footsoldiers were walking upside down. Then Donatello said, "It probably has to do with those fuzzy boots they have on." Then
Michelangelo said, "I would sure like to get my hands on their feet."
Then Donatello said, "You just gave me an idea." Then Michelangelo
got the footsoldiers. Score: Two, turtles. Bad guys, zippo.

★ ★ ★

Melanie
Five years, two months

Once upon a time there was a Ninja Turtle. Then April came. They went to go fight Shredder. Then they went to fight Bebop. Then April took the pizza out of the oven. Then they ate it. Then they went to fight Shredder again. Then the leftover pizza was starting to blow up. Then Raphael and Michelangelo came home. They tried to stop the pizza by shooting it with a gun. But it didn't work. Then the Ninja Turtle sewer was on fire. They tried to get out but they couldn't. The door was locked and Shredder had the keys. Then Raphael called April on the radio and said, "Get the keys from Shredder." Then she got them and freed the Ninja Turtles from the sewer. The End.

Real-Life Events

Jeanine
Two years, five months

Dorothy giving pizza to the kids!
Sausage.
Eat it all up.
"More pizza!"
The End.

Magic

Johnny
Four years, six months
(Told at the start of the Persian Gulf crisis, 1991)

Army Guys

Once they found a bad guy and they threw their hand grenades at the bad guy. Then they came too close because they were magic and couldn't die. Then there were more bad guys and they weren't magic and they killed them. Then there were more bad guys and they weren't magic and they died, too. There is a Good Iraq and a Bad Iraq. Then they were shooting all over the place. There is still shooting all over. Then some nice Army jets came and shot the bad Army jets.

Leaving Home

Chad
Four years, six months
(Based on the book I'll Love You Forever *by Robert Munsch)*

Once upon a time there was a baby and he was two years old. And he grew and grew and grew till he was nine years old. And he never wanted to take a bath. And then he grew and grew and grew until he was a teenager. And he had wild friends.

And he grew and grew and grew till he was grown up. Then he bought a new house. And his Mom was sick and old. And then he rocked her. And then he went upstairs and stood there for a long time. And then he went upstairs and opened the door and found a new baby. He fed the new baby. It was a girl.

And then the grandmother came back. And then they ate lunch. And then they ate dinner.

The End.

Fitting In

Lisa
Five years, ten months
(Told by a Jewish child in a classroom celebrating Christmas)

One night a girl named Jessica read a story and went to sleep. While she was asleep she didn't hear a Ho-Ho-Ho sound or tiny reindeer prancing on her roof. As you all know, the person who says Ho-Ho-Ho is Santa. Santa slid down the chimney and went into the livingroom. He put some toys under the tree and near the fireplace. Jessica woke up on Christmas morning and asked her parents who had come. The parents said, "Santa. You don't know about him?" "No," said Jessica. And she ate her breakfast and she waited for her brother Charlie. Then Charlie ate breakfast and asked Jessica, "Will you read my name on all the presents that I got?" "Well," said Jessica, "only if you let me play with you." "Okay," said Charlie. Then Jessica and Charlie opened presents. The End.

Problems in the Real World

Jamie
Five years, six months

One day there was a little boy that lived in a hut. And he wanted to drink drugs. And he asked his mom, "Can I drink drugs?" His mom said, "No." Then he asked his dad. Then he said, "No." Then he went outside. He saw some men smoking. He said, "Could I have some?" The men said, "No, it's fake." And then he went on and did find some drugs. People were selling drugs. Then he bought some. He took it home. He wanted to drink it, but his mom was coming. Then he quickly hid it under the sofa. Then he found his mom wasn't coming and he opened it and then he remembered his teacher said, "Don't drink drugs." He went back to the man and pretended like he drinked the drugs and then he threw it away. The End.

Personal History

Karen
Six years, six months

Once there was a woman named Rosie. She married a guy named Jerry. Their last name was Moore. Then Rosie went to the hospital. She had a baby named Matthew Graves Moore. She said, "If this is a girl, I will name her Karen." Then Rosie went to the hospital again. She had Scott Adams Moore. Then she went to the hospital again and had Karen Meghan Moore. When Matthew grew up, he liked baseball. When Scott grew up, he loved baseball more than Matthew.

Matthew and Scott played with Karen all the time. Then Karen learned how to walk her first step. She said, "Goo, goo, gah, gah."

Now that Karen grew up, she met a friend named Megan. Megan and Karen play a lot. Megan has a friend named Julia.

Karen has a cat named Oliver.

Matthew traded baseball cards with Scott. Matthew could hit a home run. Scott tried, too. He only could hit the ball. Scott hated New Kids on the Block.

Megan and Karen and Julia were in Daisy Girl Scouts together. They learned their sign.

The End.

The Continuing Adventures Of . . .

Gloria
Five years, six months

CHAPTER FOUR. They had spent all night looking for food. They took another day to look for the food. And finally, just before the sun was getting ready to set, they saw a big, tall palm tree with lots of leaves on it. Below it they saw hundreds and hundreds of fresh green palm leaves. Then they ran up and stuffed all of the palm leaves into their bags.

They went back home to the camping spot.

They all climbed into their sleeping bags. Then Karin said, "All right, remember the time I changed into a unicorn?" And they all yelled, "Yeah, we remember that. That was really exciting." Then Karin said, "Guess what! I can share my abilities for one night only each week." And they said, "Can we do that tonight?" Karin said, "Of course!"

Then Karin said, "Lie down. Now we've all got to hold hands," and Karin used her magic and they all turned into unicorns. But what was really strange and funny was that when they changed into unicorns, they all ended up at the bottom of their sleeping bags!

The End.

Sample Transcripts of Dictation

Below are children's stories, followed by transcripts of tape recordings of the actual storytelling and dictation. The sessions were taped to give the teachers another view of the process and help them understand it better.

Julie Oudin
Toddler teacher

Mary's Story

Mommy and Daddy are going on an airplane. Last night they went on an airplane. The airplane took them back home. They sleep with me in my bed. The End.

The Transcript

(Mary comes to the table as the teacher sits down. She is holding Bert and Ernie dolls.)

JULIE: Okay, you can put Bert and Ernie on the table. You want to tell me a story today. Let me get the paper ready.

MARY: Mommy and Daddy going on airplane.

JULIE: Okay, Mary. Let me get set. Remember your story. I'll put your name on the paper and then I can copy that sentence. Mary, January 19. Mommy and Daddy going on an airplane?

MARY: *(Nods.)*

JULIE: Mommy and Daddy are going on an airplane.

MARY: I want to act it out on the floor.

JULIE: Wait a minute. You want to act it out on the floor? We will! Mommy and Daddy are going on an airplane. There you go.

MARY: *(Points to artwork on board.)* Look at that tree.

JULIE: I see the trees, but let's get back to the story. You want to tell me about Mommy and Daddy on the airplane. Where are they going?

MARY: Last night they go on an airplane.

JULIE: Last night they went on an airplane?

MARY: (*Nods several times.*)

JULIE: Last night they went on an airplane. (*To another student:* Good morning, Dan, come on in. Come on in.) Mary, where did the airplane take them?

MARY: Uh, to get Karen.

JULIE: To get Karen?

MARY: Karen, *Karen!*

JULIE: Who's Karen?

MARY: Cabin.

JULIE: Cabin? To a cabin? I'm not understanding. Let me try again. Where did the airplane take them? (*Although what Mary was trying to tell the teacher was clear, on the tape, the teacher misunderstood her during the dictation process. Interestingly, Mary seemed to change her intended story as a result.*)

MARY: Uhh to . . . uhh . . . back home.

JULIE: The airplane took them back home?

MARY: Yeah.

JULIE: The airplane took them back home. What happened when they got home, Mary?

MARY: (*Smiles and turns away as Ashley comes in.*)

JULIE: Oh, I know you're happy to see Ashley come in, but let's get back to your story because you're at the story table now. What happened after they came home?

MARY: They sleep with me.

JULIE: They sleep with Mary? They sleep with Mary in her bed? They sleep with me in my bed?

MARY: Yeah.

JULIE: They sleep with me in my bed. Mary, let me read to you what you've written. Mommy and Daddy are going on an airplane. Last night they went on an airplane. The airplane took them back home. They sleep with me in my bed. Is there more to your story?

MARY: No.

JULIE: Should I write "The End"?

MARY: Yeah.

JULIE: Yes, okay. The End. That's a great story. We'll act it out on the carpet.

★   ★   ★

Monica Rascoe
Pre-kindergarten teacher

Ali's Story

Me and my mom and my dad went in to the car to go to Wes's to eat. And I ordered a hot dog and got a root beer to drink. Michael got to sit in a booster seat and so did I. And I was swinging on the bar at the restaurant while I was waiting for my food. And two boys saw me swinging and they decided to swing. Then their mom got angry because she wanted them to sit in their own seat. Their mom made them sit in their own seats. And I got to sit next to the boys to eat. Then we went home. I asked if we could have a fire but my dad said that there was enough wood but he wanted to save the wood for a real cold day. And then my mom read stories to me and then she tickled me and then I fell asleep. The End.

The Transcript

MONICA: Let's see. A-l-i.

ALI: No.

MONICA: Oh, you wanted to write it? Do you want to write next to it? Do you want to go ahead and write Ali next to it?

ALI: Ali, Ali. The name is Ali Ali.

MONICA: Yeah, that would be like Ali Ali. All right. Do you know what your last name is, Ali?

ALI: Yes.

MONICA: And what is it?

ALI: Parks.

MONICA: And that's spelled P-a-r-k-s.

ALI: I don't like that on there.

MONICA: You don't like that on there? I won't put it on next time then. Okay. January 10. How do you want your story to begin?

ALI: (*Silence.*)

MONICA: Are you going to write a real story or a pretend story?

ALI: I don't know.

MONICA: Do you want to start, "Once upon a time"?

ALI: (*Silence.*)

MONICA: (*Talks to other children.*) Okay, Ali.

ALI: Me, my mom and dad and Michael went in the car to go eat some dinner.

MONICA: My mom, my dad, and Michael went in the car to go eat for dinner?

ALI: Yes.

MONICA: . . . Went in the car . . .

ALI: . . . To go to Wes's . . .

MONICA: Wes's? I've never been there, is it good?

ALI: Yes.

MONICA: . . . To eat. Okay.

ALI: And . . . I ordered a hot dog and . . .

MONICA: I ordered a hot dog and . . .

ALI: I got root beer to drink.

MONICA: I ordered a hot dog and got root beer to drink. Yum,
           sounds good.

ALI: And . . . Michael got to sit in a booster, so did I.

MONICA: Michael got to sit in a booster seat and so did I. You like
           to sit in a booster seat?

ALI: So I'll be high. And I was swinging on the bar.

MONICA: At the restaurant?

ALI: While I was waiting for my food.

MONICA: And I was swinging on the bar at the restaurant.

ALI: While I was waiting for my food.

MONICA: And I was swinging on the bar at the restaurant.

ALI: While I was waiting for my food.

MONICA: I was waiting for my food. Um, you were swinging on the
           bar? They had a bar at the restaurant you could swing on?
           For kids to swing on?

ALI: It was where you stay inside and order but I was just swinging on it.

MONICA: Oh, it wasn't really there for kids to swing on, but you were, and it was fun. . . . And then two boys saw me swinging and they came . . . and they decided to swing. Or they came on swinging?

ALI: They decided to.

MONICA: They decided to swing. What else happened at the restaurant?

ALI: And then the mom got angry because, 'cause the mom wanted them to sit in their own seat.

MONICA: Angry because she wanted them to sit on their own seats?

ALI: Yeah.

MONICA: Did they do what their mom wanted them to do?

ALI: Yes.

MONICA: Do you want to write that in the story? Okay, how shall we say that? It says, and then . . .

ALI: Their mom made them do it.

MONICA: Okay, and their mom got angry because she wanted them to sit in their own seat. Their mom made them?

ALI: Their mom made them.

MONICA: Their mom made them. Okay.

ALI: Sit in their seats.

MONICA: Sit in their own seats. Okay, all righty. What happened after that?

ALI: And I got to sit next to them.

MONICA: To whom?

ALI: To the boys.

MONICA: And I got to sit . . .

ALI: To eat.

MONICA: Next to the boys? The boys, the boys, to eat? What were their names? Did you know their names?

ALI: No.

MONICA: Okay, and I got to sit next to the boys to eat. I bet that was fun.

ALI: And I asked if we could make a fire, but my dad said we didn't have enough wood, so we didn't make a fire.

MONICA: I asked if we could have a fire? Have a fire, but my dad said there wasn't enough . . .

ALI: My dad said there *was* enough wood, but he wanted to wait for a real cold day.

MONICA: My dad said there was enough wood, but he wanted to wait until a real cold day? But he wanted to save it? For a real cold day? To save the wood for a real cold day? The wood for a real cold day. How do you want this story to end? We're just getting to the end.

ALI: And then me and my mom read stories, and then she tickled me. Then I went to bed.

MONICA: Then me and my mom read stories and she tucked me into bed?

ALI: No, and then she tickled me. . . . Then I fell asleep.

MONICA: Then she tickled me and then I fell asleep? And then I fell asleep. Okay. The End? The End.

★   ★   ★

Mary Seidel
Pre-kindergarten teacher

Steven's Story

Once upon a time there was a hunter. He was hunting and then he found something. He found a rabbit's hole-nest. And then a rabbit jumped out and it was Bugs Bunny. Daffy Duck flew over the rabbit. He was going south. Then the bunny got frozen like an ice cube. And then the spring came. And then the bunny could go south. And then Daffy Duck can pick Bugs Bunny up so they can have another short way to go to the south. The End.

The Transcript

MARY: Steven, today is January, what's the number of the day? Twenty-four. All right, what kind of story would you like to tell?

STEVEN: That one right here.

MARY: Okay. What story do you want to tell today?

STEVEN: (*Mumbles.*)

MARY: Hum?

STEVEN: Once upon a time . . .

MARY: Once . . . that's a good way to start a story . . . upon a time. Okay.

STEVEN: There was . . .

MARY: There was . . . All right.

STEVEN: A hunter.

MARY: There was a hunter? There was a hunter. Okay. Okay, what did the hunter do?

STEVEN: He was hunting.

MARY: He was hunting. Okay. He was hunting, that's what hunters do, don't they? He was hunting. All right.

STEVEN: And then he found something.

MARY: And then he found something. Okay.

STEVEN: Let's see. I don't know what.

MARY: What?

STEVEN: He found a rabbit hole.

MARY: He found a rabbit's nest.

STEVEN: No. No. A rabbit's hole-nest.

MARY: He found a rabbit's hole-nest. Okay. (*To another child:* You can sit with her and listen. Hi.) He found a rabbit's hole-nest. Great!

STEVEN: Then a rabbit jumped up—then a rabbit jumped out of the hole—Bugs Bunny.

MARY: And then a rabbit jumped out and it was Bugs Bunny.

STEVEN: And Daffy Duck flew over the rabbit.

MARY: Daffy . . . (*To another child:* It doesn't work too well? You know what? If it doesn't work you can put the top on and throw it into the garbage can. Thanks for telling me, Alex.) Daffy Duck—what did he do?

STEVEN: Daffy Duck flew over the rabbit.

MARY: Flew over the rabbit. Where was he going?

STEVEN: You mean Daffy Duck?

MARY: Yeah.

STEVEN: He was going in the south.

MARY: Okay. He . . . that's what birds do in the winter, isn't it? He was going south.

STEVEN: Then the winter got frozen. Then the bunny got frozen like an ice cube.

MARY: Then the bunny got frozen like an ice cube. Oooh! Then the bunny got frozen like an ice cube. Poor bunny.

STEVEN: And then the bunny and then the ice cube melted.

MARY: Okay. And then the bunny could go south. Was he pretty cold?

STEVEN: What?

MARY: Was he pretty cold? (*Steven nods.*) Yeah. Is that why he wanted to go south? (*Steven nods.*) Yeah.

STEVEN: And then Daffy Duck can pick Bugs Bunny up so they can have another short way to go to the south.

MARY: Okay. That I didn't hear. Then what? Then Daffy Duck . . .

STEVEN: Picked up the rabbit.

MARY: Okay.

STEVEN: To have a short way to—uh—south.

MARY: Okay. Picked up the rabbit to have a short way south. All right.

STEVEN: The end.

MARY: The end. Look at that. That was a long story, Steven. Thank you. The end. All right, which [copy] would you like to have? This one [the original] or this one [the carbon]?

STEVEN: Why are they both black?

MARY: Do you know why? Because my pen has black ink. Sometimes I have a pen that has blue ink, but if I use that pen the carbon paper always comes out black. Today I had a black pen. Here's your copy. Okay. Steven, do you want to read along? This is your story.

* * *

Carol Heath
Pre-kindergarten Teacher

Ryan's Story

I was a real Ninja Turtle. Then I fighted Shredder. And then Matthew H.
was Leonardo, and I was Michelangelo. We ate pizza in the sewers. Then
we went to the store and bought things to put on our pizza. And then we
ate the pizza with the stuff on it. Then we went back to fight Shredder
again. I got the Ninja Turtle garbage thrower and threw the ooze on him.
He couldn't get up. And then we went to rest in the sewers. After we took
a nap in the sewers, we ate some more pizza. And then we went to fight
Crang. And then me and Matthew threw him against the wall. Then we
threw some more retro-mutigent ooze from the garbage thrower. Then
we fought Bebop and Rock Steady and we threw them against the wall.
The End.

The Transcript

RYAN: I was a Ninja Turtle.

CAROL: All right, that's how it starts? All right, I was a Ninja
Turtle.

RYAN: I was a real Ninja Turtle.

CAROL: I was a real Ninja Turtle. Okay.

RYAN: Then I fighted Shredder.

CAROL: Then I did what to Shredder?

RYAN: Fighted him.

CAROL: Oh, can I write "I fought Shredder"?

RYAN: No, fighted.

CAROL: Okay. "Then I fighted Shredder."

RYAN: Then I fell without even looking.

CAROL: That's terrific.

RYAN: And then . . . all right. Matthew H. came and he was . . . let me change it. And Matthew H. was Leonardo.

CAROL: Matthew H. was Leonardo.

RYAN: He was the real one.

CAROL: Okay. (*She talks to another child sitting at table.*)

RYAN: And I'm Michelangelo.

CAROL: Matthew H. was Leonardo and I was Michelangelo. Okay. What did you two Ninja Turtles do? (*To another student:* Ryan, can you sit right over here? I'm a little crowded.)

RYAN: We ate pizza in the sewer.

CAROL: We ate pizza in the sewer. That's what you Ninja Turtles like to do. Then what happened?

RYAN: Then we went to the store and got some stuff on our pizza.

CAROL: Then we went to the store and did what?

RYAN: Put stuff on our pizza.

CAROL: Bought things to put on our pizza.

RYAN: Then we ate the pizza with the stuff on it.

CAROL: Then we ate the pizza with the stuff on it. Whatever happened to Shredder?

RYAN: Then we went to . . . back to fight Shredder again.

CAROL: Then we went back to fight Shredder again.

RYAN: That's what my picture looks like.

CAROL: Oh, really?

RYAN: With Matthew H. on the cover.

CAROL: Aha. Okay. What happened when you were fighting him?

RYAN: I got the Ninja Turtle garbage thrower . . .

CAROL: Wait a minute. I got the Ninja Turtle garbage thrower?

RYAN: And throwed the, threw the . . . *(tape inaudible)* . . . it was the real one, the big one.

CAROL: Oh, my gosh. I got the Ninja Turtle garbage thrower and threw the ooze? Ugh . . . the ooze on him. What did he do when you threw that ooze on him?

RYAN: Then we went out of the techni-drum and . . . to take his nap.

CAROL: But what happened to Shredder after you threw the ooze on him?

RYAN: He couldn't get out.

CAROL: Oh, I see, he couldn't get out. Was he like stuck?

RYAN: Yeah. And then we went to rest in the sewer.

CAROL: And then we went to rest in the sewers. I guess you were tired after fighting him. Huh?

RYAN: Yeah. And then after we took a nap in the sewers we went off and ate some more.

CAROL: After we took a nap in the sewers . . .

RYAN: We woke up and ate some more pizza.

CAROL: We ate . . . you guys were hungry . . . ate some more pizza.

RYAN: We eat lots of pizza, we ate three pizzas in the store.

CAROL: Oh my gosh, all right, you want me to write that right down, or were you just telling me that?

RYAN: No, I want you to write it.

CAROL: All right. After we took a nap at the sewers we ate some more pizza. We ate three pizzas? Do you want me to write that?

RYAN: No.

CAROL: No, okay. Tell me what I should write after "we ate some more pizza."

RYAN: We . . . Crang.

CAROL: Crying?

RYAN: Crang.

CAROL: Oh, Crang. And then we went to fight Crang. I don't know how to spell that, I guess I'll just guess. Do you know how to spell it? No? All right. C-r-a-n-g. How about that?

RYAN: Yes. That's how my mom spelled it.

CAROL: Okay. And then we went to fight Crang.

RYAN: And then me and Matthew H. . . . (*tape inaudible*) . . . wall.

CAROL: And then me and Matthew threw him against the wall. . . . Oooh, you guys are rough. What happened to him?

RYAN: Then we threw some more retro-mutigent ooze on him with a Ninja guard's thrower.

CAROL: Then we threw some more . . . What did you call that stuff?

RYAN: Retro-mutigent ooze.

CAROL: Retro-mutigent . . .

RYAN: Mutigent ooze.

CAROL: Ooze. . . . Or should I say *retro-mutant* ooze? I've never heard of that before.

RYAN: No.

CAROL: No. Retro-mutigent.

RYAN: Retro-mutigent ooze.

CAROL: Mutigent ooze.

RYAN: That was in the . . .

CAROL: From the garbage thrower?

RYAN: Yeah.

CAROL: Boy, oh boy. Poor Crang. Is Crang a bad guy?

RYAN: Yeah.

CAROL: Yeah. Then we threw some more retro-mutigent ooze from the garbage thrower. Think about how your story is going to end. Only a little more space.

RYAN: And then we fighted the Bebop and Rock Steady, and threw them against the wall.

CAROL: Them against the wall, too? Oh wait, say that again.

RYAN: Bebop and Rock Steady.

CAROL: Okay. Then we fought Bebop and Rock Steady, and we threw them against the wall.

RYAN: Bebop and Rock Steady.

CAROL: And we threw them against the wall. And we threw them . . .

RYAN: Against the wall.

CAROL: Against the wall.

RYAN: I want to play some.

CAROL: Is your story over?

RYAN: Yeah.

CAROL: You didn't say "The End." I didn't know. The End. Okay.

*   *   *

Roula Stefanidas
Kindergarten teacher

Kelly's Story

Once upon a time there were three little bunnies. Their house was in an old oak tree. There was a house near the tree and the people who lived there were really nice to the bunnies. And they had a cat which was named Susie. Susie went over and knocked on their door. The bunnies opened the door and went outside to play with Susie. They played all morning until it was lunch time. The people served the bunnies some carrots and then Susie and the bunnies went out to play until it was dinner time. Then the bunnies went home and the bunnies were very kind and the next morning they didn't wake up until it was dinner time. The End.

The Transcript

ROULA: Okay, Kelly, ready?

KELLY: (*Indicates yes.*)

ROULA: Let's write Kelly up at the top. And what's today's date?

KELLY: Tuesday . . .

ROULA: Tuesday. December . . .

KELLY: The fourth.

ROULA: The fourth, 1989. Okay, I'm ready.

KELLY: Once upon a time . . .

ROULA: Good start. Once upon a time . . .

KELLY: There was three little bunnies.

ROULA: There were three little bunnies. Did you do a bunny story last time?

KELLY: Yes.

ROULA: You like bunnies, don't you? Okay. There were three little bunnies.

KELLY: Their house was in an old oak tree.

ROULA: Their house was in an old oak tree.

KELLY: This was in a yard of some people that really . . . were very nice to them.

ROULA: Say that again for me now?

KELLY: There were some people that . . . there was a house near the tree.

ROULA: Okay. There was a house near the tree.

KELLY: The people that was in there was really nice to the bunnies.

ROULA: And the people who lived there were really nice to the bunnies. I guess they liked bunnies. Okay.

KELLY: And they had a cat that was named Susie.

ROULA: And they had a cat that was named . . .

KELLY: Susie.

ROULA: Susie. I like that.

KELLY: Then Susie went over to the bunnies' house and knocked on the door every single day and they played together.

ROULA: Let's start again. Susie went over to the tree? Went over and knocked on their door.

KELLY: Bunnies opened their door and they went out to play with . . .

ROULA: Bunnies opened the door and went outside . . .

KELLY: To play with Susie.

ROULA: To play with Susie. I guess cats liked to play with bunnies . . . in your story.

KELLY: I own a cat. I know his name's Susie.

ROULA: Would you like to hear the story before we continue?

KELLY: Yes.

ROULA: Once upon a time there were three little bunnies. Their house was in an old oak tree. There was a house near the tree and the people who lived there were really nice to the bunnies. And they had a cat which was named Susie. Susie went over and knocked on their door. The bunnies opened the door and went outside to play with Susie.

KELLY: And they played all day until it was lunch time.

ROULA: They played all day . . .

KELLY: Morning.

ROULA: Oh, you'd like to say morning? I'll change that . . . all morning until it was lunch time.

KELLY: They ate, the people served the bunnies some carrots for lunch.

ROULA: Okay. They ate lunch with the people? Okay. The people served the bunnies some carrots? Did the people eat carrots also?

KELLY: No.

ROULA: No, okay.

KELLY: Then they and then Susie and the bunnies went out to play until it was dinner time.

ROULA: And then Susie and the bunnies went out to play until it was dinner time.

KELLY: Then the bunnies went home.

ROULA: Then the bunnies went home.

KELLY: And the bunnies (*tape inaudible*).

ROULA: And the bunnies went home and the bunnies were very kind. And the next morning . . . what did they do?

KELLY: The next morning they stayed in bed from a long time in bed.

ROULA: They did what?

KELLY: They didn't wake up until it was dinner time.

ROULA: Oh, and the next morning they didn't wake up until it was dinner time? Wow, they must have been really tired.

KELLY: (*Indicates yes.*)

ROULA: And the next morning they didn't wake up until it was dinner time.

KELLY: The End.

ROULA: The End.

Books and Stories Children Like to Dramatize

This is a sample list of books recommended by teachers who dramatize stories with children on a regular basis.

Vingananee and the Tree Toad, a Liberian Tale	Verna Aardema
Who Sank the Boat?	Pamela Allen
All Night, All Day	Ashley Bryan
Shiko and His Eight Wicked Brothers	Ashley Bryan
Mr. Gumpy's Motorcar	John Burningham
Mr. Gumpy's Outing	John Burningham
Hey! Get Off Our Train	John Burningham
The Grouchy Ladybug	Eric Carle
Rooster's Off to See the World	Eric Carle
Bony-Legs	Joanna Cole
The Large and Growly Bear	Gertrude Crampton
The Legend of the Bluebonnet	Tomie de Paola
The Legend of the Indian Paintbrush	Tomie de Paola
Play with Me	Marie Ets
Hattie and the Fox	Mem Fox
The Chick and the Duckling	Mirra Ginsburg
The Gunniwolf	Wilhelmina Harper
Chrysanthemum	Kevin Henkes
Ben's Trumpet	Rachel Isadora
The Snowy Day	Ezra Jack Keats
Letter to Amy	Ezra Jack Keats
Peter's Chair	Ezra Jack Keats
Geraldine's Blanket	Holly Keller
Anansi and the Moss-Covered Rock	Eric Kimmel
The Carrot Seed	Ruth Krauss
The Story of Ferdinand	Munro Leaf
Tacky the Penguin	Helen Lester
How Many Spots Does a Leopard Have?	Julius Lester
Frederick	Leo Lionni
The Elves and the Shoemaker	Freya Littledale
The Magic Fish	Freya Littledale
Anasi the Spider, a Tale from the Ashanti	Gerald McDermott

Brown Bear, Brown Bear	Bill Martin, Jr.
Listen to the Rain	Bill Martin, Jr. & John Archambault
Me, Too!	Mercer Mayer
Stone Soup	Ann McGovern
Too Much Noise	Ann McGovern
Snow Lion	David McPhail
The Funny Little Woman	Arlene Mosel
Mortimer	Robert Munsch
50 Degrees below Zero	Robert Munsch
Show and Tell	Robert Munsch
One Potato	Sue Porter
Relatives Came	Cynthia Rylant
The Little Band	James Sage
Abiyoyo	Pete Seeger
Where the Wild Things Are	Maurice Sendak
The King's Choice	K. Shivkumar
Caps for Sale	Esphyr Slobodkina
The Mitten	Alvin Tresselt
Two Foolish Cats	Yoshiko Uchida
Mouse Count	Ellen Stoll Walsh
Albert's Toothache	Barbara Williams
The Napping House	Audrey Wood
King Bidgood's in the Bathtub	Audrey Wood

Fairy tales such as "The Gingerbread Man," "The Little Red Hen," and "The Twelve Dancing Princesses" provide rich material for the children's own stories. Paul Galdone's Ladybird editions of these stories, or other retellings for younger readers are best for dramatization.

Folk tales and legends often make for successful dramas, and also expose the children to other cultures. Look in anthologies of Native American and African stories such as *The Keepers of the Earth* by Michael J. Caduto and Joseph Bruchac, and *In the Beginning* and *The People Could Fly* by Virginia Hamilton.

Children's songs that have been made into books such as *Go Tell Aunt Rhody* by Aliki are particularly popular with children under three. Also, the following books are effective with this age group: *Tickle, Tickle; Clap Hands; All Fall Down,* and *Say Goodnight* by Helen Oxenbury; *Daddy and I* and *I Make Music* by Eloise Greenfield; and *My Sister and Me at the Beach* and *Our Day* by Lucy Dickens.

Related Classroom Literacy Activities

Here are three other activities that teachers have found extremely valuable in stimulating very young children's interest in reading and writing, while also addressing a practical or emotional need.

The Sign-in Sheet

The sign-in sheet is a kind of attendance record. It enables children under six to have a regular and meaningful opportunity to write their names. This is especially valuable for three- to five-year-olds, who may be just learning to form letters. "Signing in" places name writing in a context that not only affords the children practice, but also the opportunity to observe and think about the meaning and letters of other children's names. I recommend a computer-generated name sheet with the list of names pre-printed in oversized letters, and plenty of room to sign in next to them. The sign-in table should be placed near the door, and should have at least three or four different pens or pencils available to choose from.

The Turn-Taking Sheet

The turn-taking sheet functions similarly to the sign-in sheet, in that it keeps a record of something necessary to classroom life. It is slightly more advanced than the sign-in sheet because it is used spontaneously, and does not offer model names from which to copy. Simply, children sign up for a chance at activities or materials that require taking turns (a new book, the computer, first on line to the cafeteria, etc.). In the beginning, the teacher can write a heading (such as Cafeteria Line) and perhaps draw a picture, but eventually this responsibility can be transferred to the children themselves, especially kids five and older.

Kid News

Kid News is a very popular activity with three- to eight-year-olds, and is another way of allowing children their say. Kid News is easy to do. The teacher writes down the children's news, usually in large print on oversized paper, and then displays it for the day. Some teachers take one item of news per child each day. This can be quite time-consuming in large classes, however. Other teachers limit the news to three or four children per day. They also maintain a News turn-taking list.

The value of Kid News to reading and writing development is greatly enhanced when it is taken on a daily basis, usually during the morning Circle Time or opening exercises. It gives the children an opportunity to see their thoughts in large print, which can be easily memorized, and then "read" back. Houston teacher Connie Floyd made the observation that for children below first grade, telling news aloud is similar to classroom journal writing. Its social dimensions, however, play right into the developmental needs of these younger children.

Bibliography of Works Cited

Atwell, Nancie. "Bringing It All Back Home." *The New Advocate*, vol. 2, no. 1 (1989).

Boyer, Ernest L. *Ready to Learn*. Princeton, N.J.: Carnegie Foundation for the Advancement of Teaching, 1991.

Coles, Robert. *The Call of Stories*. Boston: Houghton Mifflin, 1989.

Dewey, John. *Schools of Tomorrow*. New York: E.P. Dutton, 1915.

Donaldson, Margaret. *Children's Minds*. New York: W.W. Norton, 1978.

Egoff, Sheila, ed. *Only Connect*. Toronto: Oxford University Press, 1969.

Goodman, Ken. *What's Whole in Whole Language*. Portsmouth, N.H.: Heinemann, 1986.

Holt, John. *Learning All the Time*. New York: Addison-Wesley, 1989.

Kozol, Jonathan. *Savage Inequalities*. New York: HarperCollins, 1991.

McLane, Joan B., and McNamee, Gillian D. *Early Literacy*. Cambridge, Mass.: Harvard University Press, 1990.

Olsen, Tillie. *Tell Me a Riddle*. New York: Dell, 1960.

Paley, Vivian. *The Boy Who Would Be a Helicopter*. Cambridge, Mass.: Harvard University Press, 1990.

_____. *Wally's Stories*. Cambridge, Mass.: Harvard University Press, 1981.

_____. *You Can't Say You Can't Play*. Cambridge, Mass.: Harvard University Press, 1992.

Raines, Shirley C., and Canady, Robert J. *The Whole Language Kindergarten*. New York: Teachers College Press, 1990.

Smith, Frank. *Reading without Nonsense*. New York: Teachers College Press, 1985.

Strickland, Dorothy, and Morrow, Lesley Mandell, eds. *Emerging Literacy: Young Children Learn to Read and Write*. Newark, Del.: International Reading Assoc., 1989.

Teale, William H. "Toward a Theory of How Children Learn to Read and Write Naturally." *Language Arts*, vol. 59, no. 6 (1982).

Teale, William H., and Sulzby, Elizabeth. *Emergent Literacy: Writing and Reading*. Norwood, N.J.: Ablex Publishing Corp., 1989.

Vygotsky, Lev S. *Mind in Society*. Cambridge, Mass.: Harvard University Press, 1978.

Children's Books

The Adventures of Babar, Antoine de Brunhoff.
Babies, Gyo Fujikawa.
Baby Ben's Bow Wow Book, Harriet Ziefert and Norman Gorbaty.
Brown Bear, Brown Bear, Bill Martin, Jr.
The Chronicles of Narnia, C.S. Lewis.
Could Be Worse, James Stevenson.
The Five Chinese Brothers, Claire Bishop.
Frog Went A-Courtin, John Langstaff and Feodor Rojankovsky.
Goodnight Moon, Margaret Wise Brown.
Heidi, Johanna Spyri.
I Am a Baby Dinosaur, Franois Crozat.
Little House (series), Laura Ingalls Wilder.
Madeline, Ludwig Bemelmans.
Pat the Bunny, Dorothy Kunhardt.
Ramona, Beverly Cleary.
Sleeping Beauty, folktale.
Snow White, Walt Disney.
Snow White and the Seven Dwarfs, folktale.
Strega Nona, Tomie de Paola.
The Three Billy Goats Gruff, folktale.
The Three Pigs, folktale.

OTHER T&W PUBLICATIONS YOU MIGHT ENJOY

The Writing Book by Inky Penguin. A creative writing workbook for students grades 3-6 that is actually fun to use. "A good book for encouraging creative writing"—*Home Education.* "Imaginative and exciting!"—Katie Whitaker.

The Teachers & Writers Handbook of Poetic Forms edited by Ron Padgett. A clear, straightforward, entertaining guide to 74 traditional and modern poetic forms. "A treasure"—*Kliatt Young Adult Paperback Book Guide.* "A solid beginning reference source for poetics"—*Choice.* "A small wonder!"—*Poetry Project.*

Playmaking: Children Writing and Performing Their Own Plays by Daniel Judah Sklar. A step-by-step account of teaching children to write, direct, and perform their own plays. Winner of the American Alliance for Theatre & Education's Distinguished Book Award. "Fascinating"—*Kliatt.*

Personal Fiction Writing by Meredith Sue Willis. A complete and practical guide for teachers of writing from elementary through college level. Contains more than 350 writing ideas. "A terrific resource for the classroom teacher as well as the novice writer"—*Harvard Educational Review.*

The List Poem: A Guide to Teaching & Writing Catalog Verse by Larry Fagin. Defines list poetry, traces its history, gives advice on teaching it, offers many writing ideas, and presents more than 200 examples by children and adults.

Origins by Sandra R. Robinson with Lindsay McAuliffe. A new way to get students excited about language: by introducing them to the fascination of word origins. "Refreshing and attractive"—Robert MacNeil. "Highly recommended"—*Library Materials Guide.* "Exciting and imaginative"—*The Children's Advocate.*

The Poetry Connection: An Anthology of Contemporary Poems with Ideas to Stimulate Children's Writing by Nina Nyhart and Kinereth Gensler. "An entirely indispensable classroom tool"—*California Poets-in-the-Schools.*

Moving Windows by Jack Collom. An in-depth guide to evaluating the poetry children write. "A landmark book . . . stimulating ideas that any teacher could utilize and wonderful examples of children's poems"—*Oregon English.*

The Writing Workshop, Vols. 1 & 2 by Alan Ziegler. A perfect combination of theory, practice, and specific assignments. "Invaluable to the writing teacher"—*Contemporary Education.*

The Whole Word Catalogue, Vols. 1 & 2. T&W's best-selling guides to teaching imaginative writing. "*WWC 1* is probably the best practical guide for teachers who really want to stimulate their students to write"—*Learning.*

•

For a complete and free catalogue of T&W books, magazines, audiotapes, videotapes, and computer writing games, contact Teachers & Writers Collaborative, 5 Union Square West, New York, NY 10003–3306, tel. (212) 691-6590.